LIVING
by FAITH
STUART BLANCH

WILLIAM B. EERDMANS PUBLISHING COMPANY
GRAND RAPIDS, MICHIGAN

© 1983 Stuart Blanch
First published in 1983 by
Darton, Longman and Todd Ltd., London

This American edition published 1984 through special arrangement with Darton, Longman and Todd by Wm. B. Eerdmans Publishing Company, 255 Jefferson Ave. S.E., Grand Rapids, Mich. 49503

All rights reserved
Printed in the United States of America

Library of Congress Cataloging in Publication Data

Blanch, Stuart Y. (Stuart Yarworth)
Living by faith.

Includes index.
1. Faith.   2. Christian life — Anglican authors.
3. Blanch, Stuart Y. (Stuart Yarworth)   I. Title.
BT771.2.B59   1984   234'.2   84-10182
ISBN 0-8028-0008-4

CONTENTS

PREFACE

To attempt a book called 'Living by Faith' calls for a certain element of autobiography. A book at least twice as large could have been written but I have concentrated deliberately on aspects of faith of which I have some personal, though no doubt elementary experience. However, in each chapter I have attempted to enlarge my own area of awareness by calling on the resources of Holy Scripture and on other authors better equipped than I am in this particular field. The autobiographical sections will, I trust, do no one any harm and I am grateful to those who unwittingly have provided living illustrations of the theme.

I am indebted to the publishers for their invitation to write a book which I would never have written otherwise, and in particular to Lesley Riddle for helping me over the planning and the completion stages. I am indebted also to David Blunt, Daphne Wood and Val Smith, who have been responsible for producing the final script. I am indebted to many of whom I am aware who have helped me in my particular pilgrimage, and many others of whom I am not aware at all. Finally, my supreme debt is to my wife Brenda with whom I have shared this life of faith for the last forty years. This book is dedicated to her as a token of my love and gratitude.

STUART BLANCH
Bishopthorpe, York
February 1983

Acknowledgements

Thanks are due to the following for permission to reproduce extracts from copyright sources.

Gerald Duckworth and Co. Ltd: *Jesus and the Constraints of History* by A. E. Harvey.

Extracts from *The Collected Poems of Edwin Muir* reprinted by permission of Faber and Faber Ltd and Oxford University Press, New York.

Macmillan, London and Basingstoke and Alfred A. Knopf Inc: *A Distant Mirror: The Calamitous 14th Century* by Barbara Tuchman.

Penguin Books Ltd: *Revelations of Divine Love* by Julian of Norwich, tr. Clifton Wolters. *The Confessions of Saint Augustine*, tr. R. S. Pine-Coffin. *Pelican History of the World* by J. M. Roberts.

SCM Press and Harper and Row Inc: *Theology of Hope* by Jurgen Moltmann.

The majority of Scripture quotations in this publication are from the Revised Standard Version of the Bible, copyrighted 1971 and 1952 by the Division of Christian Education of the National Council of the Churches of Christ in the USA.

INTRODUCTION

The history of this book started a long time ago. From 1952 to 1957 I was a country parish priest in north Oxfordshire, enjoying all the excitements of a first benefice, enthusiastic, confident, naive. I received a message one morning from my Roman Catholic colleague on the other side of the road (there was no telephone in the vicarage) asking me to call on a parishioner already well known to me. She was a woman crippled with arthritis, wholly dependent upon a devoted husband and son by whom she had to be lifted out of her bed and brought down in the morning to sit in front of the fire and then when they returned lifted again and taken up to bed. She was a woman of indomitable spirit and no little insight into the affairs of the village. I went to see her after lunch. She said to me, 'I wish you had come earlier, Vicar, because this morning I had a vision of Jesus Christ standing in front of me and saying to me "Stand up and walk".' Every parish priest will have known moments like that when his heart feels like a stone within him. 'But', she said, 'there is no one else in the house and I was afraid that if I stood up I would fall into the fire. So what do I do now?' As a minister of the Gospel, with ample illustrations and encouragements from the Gospels themselves, I ought to have been able to say something like this – 'If Jesus spoke to you this morning then there is no reason why He should not speak to you again this afternoon. In the name of Jesus Christ stand up and walk.' But I looked at that twisted frame and those shrunken limbs and that hollow face, and I could not find it in me to say the words of liberation. So the visit degenerated into a conversation, a reading from the Bible and a prayer together. When I left she remained still in her chair looking into the fire and waiting for her husband to return, resuming, after this brief experience, the old routines, and I returned home somewhat chastened, less confident and pondering on the mysterious impulse which could have turned intellectual convictions into dynamic action.

I have, off and on, been pondering that question ever since. I did not doubt the power of our Lord to heal by seemingly miraculous means in His life on earth. I did not doubt that His power to heal was now vested in those who were called to be His apostles. I had evidence enough in my own experience already to know that the lame could walk, the deaf could hear, and the blind could see, through the mighty power of the Word. What then is it that turns belief into faith, the kind of faith rehearsed, for example, in the Epistle to the Hebrews, the faith of those 'who stopped the mouths of lions, quenched the violence of fire, escaped the edge of the sword, out of weakness were made strong, waxed valiant in fight, turned to flight the armies of aliens' (11:33–4 – AV). The same kind of question is asked in that remarkable book, now unhappily out of print, *God in my Unbelief* by J. W. Stevenson (Collins, 1960). After a not dissimilar experience to mine, he says, 'Something cried out in me because I had not been able to mend what was broken – like the cry of the disciples "Why could we not cast him out".'

This book will not be concerned with systems of belief. The reader will look in vain for a cogent exposition of Christian orthodoxy. He will occasionally have to be exposed to the rigours of academic argument. The argument will have in view only a keener perception of the theology which lies behind the practical experience of the people of God, Jewish and Christian. There will be elements of autobiography, not altogether concealed, because I can only speak out of experience even though that experience has to be checked and sometimes qualified by the experience of others, as that is exhibited in the pages of the Bible.

Those who come to this book without anything that they would describe as a personal Christian experience need not for that reason close the book at this point. As we shall see in the next chapter, faith of the dynamic kind, described by the writer to the Hebrews, was not confined to the Jew or the Christian, or to the member of any other religious body. There are indeed many examples of 'secular faith' every bit as impressive in their way as the faith revealed in Sacred Scriptures. Faith could be a universal element in the moral and psychic structure of the universe, capable of being deployed by many means and for many purposes. It may be the most important hidden factor in all human experience. 'Faith', said Jesus, 'can move a mountain', where a convoy of bulldozers would be helpless.

The reader of any book may well suppose that the author is already apprised of his conclusions and is moving step by step towards them in an orderly and predetermined way. That in fact is seldom true even in the most rigorously academic or scientific books. It is probably never true for the novelist. It would be inconceivable that Anthony Powell, for example, in his massive *Dance to the Music of Time* should have perceived more than the merest outline of his last novel *Hearing Secret Harmonies* when he set out upon his first *A Question of Upbringing*. In my case, I set out in faith at the behest of my publisher and under the pressure of a contract. There is biblical precedent for this method – 'Abraham went out not knowing whither he went.'

THE FAITH OF KARL MARX

He was genuinely convinced that the process of history was both inevitable and, despite setbacks, progressive, and this intense belief excluded all possibility of doubt or disillusionment on fundamental issues.

Isaiah Berlin (*Karl Marx*, OUP, 4th edn 1978)

1 THE IMPORTANCE OF FAITH

It is sometimes supposed that faith is the private peculiarity of those who happen to belong to some religious communion – Jewish, Christian, Moslem, Buddhist, Hindu. Such faith, so it is further supposed, is little more than some adherence to some cultural system, a product of steady conditioning at home or in society at large, or at best a set of intellectual beliefs erected on a long and largely impenetrable tradition. 'Faith', the cynic says, 'is believing what you know to be untrue.' But the cynic is not alone in his attitude. The devout churchman may feel himself isolated within an arcane mystery which he cannot share and cannot expect others to understand. But a few moments' reflection will show that faith is not confined to a fortunate or deluded few but is something which underlies the everyday experience of every human being all the time.

When I catch the 125 train to London I express thereby a touching faith in men, machines and procedures, of which I know nothing and which I am wholly unable to check for myself. I believe, though I cannot prove, that the track workers have done their job, that the mechanics have tested the wheels, that the signals are working, that the engine driver is sober – and indeed that every other engine driver of every other train operating in the system is sober too. This is a huge act of faith which I share with my fellow travellers as we eat our breakfast and read our newspapers and master our files.

Such a faith is evinced even more clearly when I sit strapped in at the end of the airport runway. Did the engineer check the gauges when the aircraft was re-fuelled? Did the fitter ensure that doors of the hold were closed? On this icy morning, did they use the right de-icing mixture for the leading edges of the wings? Has the pilot recovered from the row with his wife on the previous day? Does Air Traffic Control have the lanes clear and the heights established? Does the Met. Office know of that fabulous thunderstorm brewing up in the west? And yet we sit there reading our safety procedures, listening to that 'take off' music and conversing with our neighbours, trusting (if that is the word) that every employee throughout the whole process of the building of the aeroplane and its maintenance has done his job with impeccable accuracy. We believe what we cannot prove – and believe it sufficiently to stake our lives on it. The man who sits in the dentist's chair or lies on the operating table, who drives his car out of the garage after a major service, sits, lies, drives by faith. Indeed, so far is it from being a private fantasy that the man who would live without faith cannot live at all. Lack of faith is a deadly privation. Faith is a commonplace.

But these are trivial examples – although serious enough if our faith happens to have been misplaced. Modern history is full of examples of secular faith every bit as impressive in their way as their counterparts in the world of religion.

Having delivered myself of no doubt an intemperate comment on what I called the 'Grey Utopias of the Communist Bloc' I received the following morning a pained but courteous letter from someone who said I must have been conditioned by my upbringing, my social status and my religious convictions to be able to pass such a judgement. The letter arrived on the day when the newspapers were full of pictures of Russian helicopter gunships patrolling the valleys of Afghanistan in pursuit of the unwilling beneficiaries of Socialist rule. Not many days before, Keesings Contemporary Archives produced its annual report on Soviet agriculture with the familiar tale of its last disastrous decline in output. Yet my correspondent, for all that I could say or for all that the statistics prove, would go on believing to the end of her days in the Marxist/Leninist myth. I do not denigrate her faith; I applaud it as an act of heroic trust against all the evidence, although I wish it could be directed to a more reliable source.

Western history over the past forty years, throws up example after example of those who, against all the odds, continued to believe that the totalitarian governments of Eastern Europe were bringing untold benefits to those over whom they ruled. Such a faith will survive even the news of suppression of trade unions in Poland and armed violence in Gdansk. The long march of Chairman Mao, the heroic resistance of a President Tito, deserve a place within the annals of heroic faith. They moved mountains with it.

When, therefore, St Paul said, 'The life I now live I live by faith in the Son of God who loved me and gave Himself for me,' he was not setting himself apart from the world by virtue of his faith, but only by virtue of Him in whom he put his faith. St Paul lived in a world still dominated by the triumphs of Alexander the Great three centuries earlier. Alexander was not just a tyrant – he was a man genuinely moved by faith in Greek culture which he wished to indigenize throughout the length and breadth of his dominions. Paul lived in a world, and indeed was a citizen of an empire, which created the *Pax Romana* by faith in the institutions and the armed might of Rome. Paul could have lived by faith in either or both, but by virtue of a compelling experience on the road to Damascus, he lived by faith in Jesus Christ.

The world is divided therefore not between those who believe and those who do not believe, but between those who believe in the powers of the world and those who believe in the Power of God. There are examples of heroism and endurance on both sides of that line and no faith is to be despised if it issues in a genuine concern for mankind and a desire to improve our human lot. Adherents of the one view or the other may yet recognize in their seeming adversaries a kinship of faith. I shall be concerned in the rest of this book primarily with faith in the Living God but I do not thereby ignore the achievements of those whose faith has a different origin and points to a different source.

AN ACT OF SELF-SURRENDER

Faith is neither a feeling nor a mental process; it is an act of self-surrender in the dark to a God who is indeed darkness as far as our human nature is concerned. And he is darkness not because of an absence of light, but rather because we are overwhelmed by the reverberations of a light to which we are as yet unaccustomed, here in the restricted world of our own unfolding history.

Carlo Caretto (*In Search of the Beyond*, DLT 1975)

2 THE MEANING OF FAITH

When Paul said that he lived by 'faith' he presumably knew what he meant, drawing as he did upon the rich resources of his ancestral religion and upon the concepts of faith which he encountered in his own Hellenistic environment in Tarsus. But we have no such resources easily available and the word 'faith' has acquired in the course of time a wide variety of meanings. It can mean little more than credulity and as such is rightly ridiculed by the rationalist – faith in the charm which the sportsman wears around his neck, faith in quack medicine which takes no account of the constitution of the human body, faith in the press astrologer on Saturday morning as he lays out before us the events of the coming week. It is the kind of faith which touches wood and hopes for the best. For others, it means little more than a formal assent to a system of dogma or to credal forms with which they have grown up. They can say the Creed with integrity in the sense that they do not positively disbelieve in any of the Articles they recite. They go their way rejoicing in their orthodoxy, wholly uncomprehending those who do not share that particular inheritance of faith. They may call themselves Catholics, Protestants, Unitarians or Jehovah's Witnesses. Their faith depends for its strength and assistance on belonging to a tight community of those who believe much the same things as they do. For others (and these are few) faith is the outcome of a long and painful process of thought leaving them no alternative, as it would seem, but to believe in certain affirmations which they have previously ignored or despised. It was presumably in such a process of thought that Malcolm Muggeridge spoke of himself as 'praising a position I cannot uphold, enchanted by a religion I cannot believe, putting all my hope in a faith I do not have'.

I say that such are few, but there have been noteworthy

examples in the twentieth century, of whom Mr Muggeridge is one, who have come this way. But for the great majority of believing mankind the intellectual element is relatively small and it is experience that provides the clue to their faith. St Paul himself after all owed his faith, so he would say, to the blinding experience on the Damascus road which assured him of the presence and the reality of the risen Christ whom he had previously derided. These faith-creating experiences can take a variety of forms – an awareness of the presence of God in prayer, the healing of body, mind or spirit in the context of worship, or an altogether inexplicable conviction of the truth such as overcame the first disciples at Pentecost. In these examples of faith we perhaps have to include that kind of faith which is little more than youthful high spirits, or rude health or an optimistic temperament.

By what standards therefore are we to judge if we, like C. S. Lewis, find ourselves 'surprised by joy'. I have said that St Paul was able to draw upon the rich resources of his ancestral religion and upon concepts of faith current in the Hellenistic world in which he lived. We do not live in either of those worlds – they are therefore inaccessible to us, inaccessible except in so far as those worlds become explicit in the languages which they have left behind them. Our only immediate resource therefore is in the Bible where our English word 'faith' is the translation of a Hebrew word in the Old Testament and a Greek word in the New. This may seem a somewhat pedantic approach for those whose faith is already a robust and enriching factor of their everyday lives. But it is the only way now available to us of reaching back behind centuries of thought and experience to the earliest formulations of that thought and experience. Words say something about those who use them.

The word from the Hebrew scriptures which largely carries the history of the experience of faith is the word derived from a root 'a-m-n' a word more familiar to us than we might expect because it is the root from which we derive our word 'Amen'. It is the word which in its earliest stages does not require a religious meaning. It can simply mean sure, established, faithful. In Isaiah 22:23 for example you will find the phrase: 'I will fasten him as a tent peg in a sure place.' You will, I am sure, appreciate that it is almost impossible to trace the history of such a word given the uncertain dating and the varying sources of the Hebrew literature available to us. But in the end it emerges as the word by which the Hebrews conveyed what we would normally understand as faith. So Abraham 'believed in the Lord; and he counted it to him for righteousness' (Genesis 15:6). The people of Israel in the wilderness, said the psalmist, 'believed not in God and trusted not in His salvation although He commanded the skies above and opened the doors of Heaven, and rained down manna upon them to eat and gave them of the corn of Heaven' (Psalm 78:22–4). Contrariwise, at the preaching of Jonah 'the people of Nineveh believed God, and they proclaimed a fast and put on sackcloth from the greatest of them even to the least of them' (Jonah 3:5).

The normally received opinion is that this 'faith' was in the first instance an expression of corporate believing built into the life of the people of God by a series of striking deliverances at the hand of God. Only later does this collective belief achieve profound individual expression in the lives of the prophets and the writings of the psalmists and the sometimes tortured convictions of the Wisdom writers. But whether used in a collective or an individual sense, the word always meant much more than assent or credulity or an intellectual persuasion. It meant, to use a helpful phrase, 'a confident decision for God', an 'amen', as St Paul puts it, to the promises of God, an exclusive trust in God as the author of their salvation. So Isaiah's analogy proves to have been helpful. The people of Israel felt themselves secured by a huge tent peg driven in to the rugged earth of God's loving providence.

It is this concept of faith, not always of course encapsulated into a single word, which underlies so many of the narratives of the Old Testament which are otherwise puzzling to the modern reader. Why did Gideon insist on reducing his army to a mere three hundred against the forces of Midian? Because he was under obligation to put his whole trust in the might of God rather than the might of arms. Why does the author make so much of the famous story of David and Goliath in 1 Samuel 17? Because he wished to emphasize the faith implicit in David's action and explicit in his own words in his encounter with Goliath – 'You come to me with a sword, with a spear and with a javelin; but I come to you in the name of the Lord of Hosts, the God of the armies of Israel.'

Why was David so roundly condemned for what seems to us
a perfectly harmless exercise – the numbering of the people?
Because the numbering of the people was an expression of
David's pride in the size of the nation rather than in the all-
prevailing power of God. This understanding of faith runs
like a golden thread throughout the whole of Scripture, and
it is this faith which St Paul expresses when he says, 'The life
that I now live in the flesh I live by faith in the Son of God,
who loved me and gave Himself for me' (Galatians 2:20). At
that point he was indeed a Hebrew of the Hebrews although
by the same token alienated from the orthodox Judaism of
his day.

The Greek New Testament owes a great deal of its vocabulary to a Greek version of the Old Testament called The
Septuagint. That was inevitable given the fact that some of
the writers of the New Testament at least were familiar only
with the Greek version of the Old Testament and therefore
sought to communicate with their readers in its language. No
Greek word will ever catch the exact nuances of the Hebrew
word which it seeks to translate. But the word which is used
for faith in the New Testament is not a bad match. It is the
word '*pistis*' and it has history not dissimilar from the word
which it translates, '*a-m-n*'. In its use in classical Greek it
does not require a religious context. It may be used simply
for 'confidence' or 'trust' as between human beings. It only
acquired religious significance when Greek became the
language of Alexander's empire and became the lingua franca
of the whole civilized world.

In that world of multiple, competing religions and competing deities, the word 'pistis' became part of the vocabulary
of religious propaganda. It was against this background that
St Paul himself used the word – against the background of
his own religious inheritance as a Hebrew, and against the
background of the fiercely competing religions of the hellenistic world in which he lived. On the one hand, his faith was
just another faith, which he proclaimed in competition with
the many other religions of the ancient world. For him the
gods of the Greeks were nothing; the only Lord was the one
who had appeared to him from Heaven at his conversion on
the Damascus road and was known to the world as 'Jesus of
Nazareth', crucified, buried and risen. On the other hand, he
never surrendered, nor could surrender, his identity with the

old People of God by whom he had been nurtured for a substantial part of his adult life.

So, to 'live by faith', in St Paul's sense, was to live by a conviction based on the historical evidence and reinforced by his experience on the Damascus road, that there was indeed a man named Jesus, a member of his own race who taught in Galilee, called to Himself a body of disciples, healed men and women of their sicknesses, confronted the Jewish establishment in Jerusalem, was crucified, dead and buried – and on the third day rose again. This was the person who appeared to Paul on the Damascus road and this was the subject of his gospel. But this same Jesus, so he believed, was none other than the Son or the personal representative on earth of the God of Abraham, Isaac and Jacob. In his view he was not establishing a new 'faith' but expressing an old, old faith in terms of the one who in his mind had become the prime representative of it. Jesus was not just one avatar amongst others, He was the Messiah, the long-expected scion of the House of Israel who was now the only true object of faith. The God he had honoured in his days as a Jewish rabbi was indeed the God and Father of our Lord Jesus Christ.

This is inevitably a sketchy account for which I must apologize to the scholars amongst you, but it will, I hope, illustrate the subtle confluence of thought that took place in St Paul's mind. His faith was the faith of his fathers, but it became capable of being expressed in terms understood by his Greek contemporaries. It was he who transmitted to the Hellenist world that precious inheritance of Hebrew faith which is described in the Epistle to the Hebrews, and at the same time focussed it forever on the person of Jesus Christ.

And what more shall I say? For time would fail me to tell of Gideon, Barak, Samson, Jephthah, of David and Samuel and the prophets – who through faith conquered kingdoms, enforced justice, received promises, stopped the mouths of lions, quenched raging fire, escaped the edge of the sword, won strength out of weakness, became mighty in war, put foreign armies to flight. Women received their dead by resurrection. Some were tortured, refusing to accept release, that they might rise again to a better life. Others suffered mocking and scourging, and even chains and imprisonment. They were stoned, they were sawn in two, they were killed with the sword; they went about in skins of sheep and goats, destitute, afflicted, ill-treated – of whom the world was not worthy – wandering over deserts and mountains, and in dens and caves of the earth. And all these, though well attested by their faith, did not receive what was promised, since God had foreseen something better for us, that apart from us they should not be made perfect. (Hebrews 11:32–40)

Gideon, Barak, Samson, Jephthah, David, Samuel and the prophets, to mention only a few of those whom the writer to the Hebrews might have mentioned, were not credulous men inspired by a religious symbol hanging round their necks; they had no creed to assent to; they were not hearty men of the world, confident in their own powers; they were not even particularly good men; and in some cases they despised religious observances; they had no Bible to quote, no dogma to impart, no good cause to embrace. They were men who made 'a confident decision for God' and by His will and through His power did mighty acts. They were 'strangers and pilgrims on the earth of whom the world was not worthy'. Their lives and achievements are the living embodiment of a living faith.

REALMS UNKNOWN

Yet hints come to me from the realm
 unknown;
Airs drift across the twilight border-land,
Odoured with life; and as from some far strand
Sea-murmured, whispers to my heart are
 blown
That fill me with a joy I cannot speak

George MacDonald (*Diary of an Old Soul*,
                    Arthur C. Fifield, 1905)

3 SOURCES OF FAITH

When St Paul said in his Letter to the Galatians (2:20) that he was now living by faith in the Son of God who loved him and gave Himself for him, he was conscious of the fact that there had been a time in his life when he was not living by faith in the Son of God who loved him and gave Himself for him. And judging by the prominence he gave to it, the crucial transaction with God which changed the course of his life was the experience of the living Christ on the road to Damascus. It took place at a point which could be located on the map on a day which could be located in the calendar. That event is commonly designated in the Church's calendar, 'The Conversion of St Paul'. From it followed that breath-taking life of intense activity and equally intense suffering on behalf of the Christ whom he had once rejected. It is not too much to say that the event changed the course of human history, set the Church on its path to triumph in the Western World and made us what we are in twentieth-century Europe. So we could describe that event as the source of St Paul's faith. But what of those who cannot look back to such an event fixed in time and space and yet who in their own way 'conquer kingdoms, enforce justice, receive promises, stop the mouths of lions, quench raging fire, escape the edge of the sword, win strength out of weakness, become mighty in war, put foreign armies to flight'. If we would live by such a faith, where are we to find it?

I begin with a personal reminiscence which at the same time pin-points the problem and illustrates the difficulty of resolving it. In the late autumn of 1942 I was stationed at Heaton Park in Manchester. It was a large transit camp capable of accommodating ten thousand men and I, with nine thousand nine hundred and ninety-nine others, was in transit waiting to be posted to the second stage in my training

as a navigator-wireless. We had spent laborious days sitting
behind a desk and a Morse key, struggling, as we felt ineffectively, to raise our speeds to the required minimum. You can
judge our relief therefore when it was announced that the
whole camp would be cleared for Christmas and we could go
home. 'But', the warrant officer added, 'look at the notice
board to make sure you are not on the guard.' Having a name
high on the alphabet is on the whole a great advantage in
the Services. You tend to be first in the long queue for sick
parade or inoculation. You tend to be near the front on pay
parade. But on this occasion it was a singular disadvantage.
When, in obedience to the warrant officer, I did look at the
notice board, I found my name at the top of the list in charge
of the guard for the whole of Christmas week. My opinion of
warrant officers in general and of this one in particular was
violently expressed. But there was no shop-steward to cham-
pion my rights.

I went back to the nissen hut with its twenty iron beds
now vacant, stoked up the fire in the tortoise stove and
prepared for a long vigil. My duties were light, my responsibilities negligible and I had time on my hands. It rained incessantly, and the only concession to Christmas cheer was a
suspicion of turkey on Christmas Day shared with a dozen
other men in a mess designed for ten thousand people. I had
time on my hands and nothing much in my kit-bag to fill it
with. But I did have a copy of the Bible, and I turned to it
almost in desperation for some diversion. I read the gospels
several times in the course of that week. My only previous
acquaintance with them had been through hearing them read
at school assembly and in the church where I once sang as a
choirboy. This was the first time I had actually read them in
detail with my whole mind concentrated upon them. The
reading of them filled me with a sense of awe and invested
that particular Christmas with a glowing warmth that I had
hardly expected when I turned back from the main gate at
the behest of the warrant officer. I was far from being a
believer at the end of that week, but certainly I could no
longer happily be an unbeliever. 'If this is not true,' I said
to myself, 'then nothing is true.'

So I look back like St Paul to a place which still appears
on the map and to a time which was recorded in my diary
and I can say that this was the beginning of my active

Christian life which ultimately led me to ordination. What I cannot say with the same confidence is that this was the fount and source of my faith, for behind that event stretched out a life of some twenty-four years which somehow had prepared me for this moment. Why did I have a Bible anyway? Why did I choose to read it then rather than propping myself up at the bar? Why should I believe it anyway, given the serious doubts I had always expressed as a professing agnostic? It looks as if the source of my faith lay somewhere further back. I recall conversations with parish priests in the parish where I happened to live. I recall with affection a loving, fatherly vicar in whose church choir I sang. I recall certain encounters at school with school masters whom I afterwards recognized to have been practising Christians. I recall moments of sheer joy – the smell of an autumn evening, or that memorable morning when I set off from home at 5 a.m. to be near the front of the queue for the Oval Test Match. I recall intimations of reality derived from the novelist whom I greatly admired at the time, Charles Morgan. Further back still I recall warm sunlit days spent with my companionable sheepdog on the farm where I was brought up. I recall? – no, I do not, I simply record, my baptism in Blakeney Parish Church in the Forest of Dean. So the source of my faith lies beyond recollection and as I would say now, lies in the inscrutable providence of the God and Father of our Lord Jesus Christ who chose me before the world began.

I now risk the charge of turning from the ridiculous to the sublime if I allude to a book which has greatly influenced the Christian church and many outside it as well – the *Confessions of St Augustine*. Augustine was bishop of an unassuming town of Hippo in a little regarded province of the Roman Empire in Africa. He was not the grand potentate that we sometimes associate with episcopacy. As Van der Meer says of him in his book *Augustine the Bishop* (Sheed and Ward, 1961):

He was hardly more than a sort of episcopal Dean and a great deal of his work was that of an ordinary priest. He was the kind of Bishop whom the more casual officials cheerfully kept waiting in their ante-rooms. There was in fact beneath the genius a very humdrum Augustine who lived in what was really a large but very ordinary presby-

tery and who could be approached by anybody about pretty
well any business that his caller fancied.

That is true but observe the words 'beneath the genius'. His
theological works are written out of the heart of his pastoral
experience in Hippo and have dominated Western theology
for centuries. But the secret of that dominance lies perhaps
less in these great theological works than in the so-called
'confessions'. I say 'so-called' because his 'confession'
contains the more primitive sense of profession of faith rather
than confession of sins. Read in a modern translation (such
as the one by R. S. Pine-Coffin, published in the Penguin
Classics, 1970) they have an immediacy which challenges
attention and which bears upon the subject of this chapter –
namely, the sources of faith. This is the account of his 'Damascus road':

> I was asking myself these questions, weeping all the while
> with the most bitter sorrow in my heart, when all at once
> I heard the singing voice of a child in a nearby house.
> Whether it was the voice of a boy or a girl I cannot say,
> but again and again it repeated the refrain 'Take it and
> read, take it and read'. At this I looked up, thinking hard
> whether there was any kind of game in which children used
> to chant words like these, but I could not remember ever
> hearing them before. I stemmed my flood of tears and stood
> up, telling myself that this could only be a divine command
> to open my book of Scripture and read the first passage on
> which my eyes should fall. For I had heard the story of
> Antony, and I remembered how he had happened to go
> into a church while the Gospel was being read and had
> taken it as a counsel addressed to himself when he heard
> the words 'Go home and sell all that belongs to you. Give
> it to the poor, and so the treasure you have shall be in
> heaven; then come back and follow me.' By this divine
> pronouncement he had at once been converted to you.
>   So I hurried back to the place where Alypius was sitting,
> for when I stood up to move away I had put down the
> book containing Paul's Epistles. I seized it and opened it,
> and in silence I read the first passage on which my eyes
> fell: 'Not in revelling and drunkenness, not in lust and
> wantonness, not in quarrels and rivalries. Rather, arm

yourselves with the Lord Jesus Christ; spend no more thought on nature and nature's appetites.' I had no wish to read more and no need to do so. For in an instant, as I came to the end of the sentence, it was as though the light of confidence flooded into my heart and all the darkness of doubt was dispelled.

This is hardly a Damascus road experience – no vision of the risen Christ, no voice from Heaven, but the monotonous tones of a child, 'Take and read, take and read'. But it marks the end of a long and painful moral and spiritual education and the beginning of a lifetime of Christian service which was to take him ultimately to the Diocese of Hippo. But he would recollect, as indeed he does so in his Confessions, the unceasing prayers of his mother for his salvation. He would recollect that creative encounter with the great Ambrose, Bishop of Milan. He would recollect those years of seeming confidence as a young man – 'in public we were cock-sure, in private superstitious and everywhere void and empty', and he would recollect the challenge to his own self-sufficiency in the death of a much-loved, familiar friend. He would recollect the mistress with whom he lived for so many years and the child that she had given him. He would recollect the wasted efforts, the pursuit of academic distinction, the arguments with the philosophers, his brief conversion to the Manichees. And in all these things he could still say, 'Through clouds of smoke God saw a spark of good faith in me' (Book IV). Whence then the source of this faith, save in the inscrutable providence of the God and Father of our Lord Jesus Christ by which this arrogant young man, so full of his own importance, so weighed down with the sins of the flesh, had his feet set on the way that led to truth and to Hippo.

The experience in the gospels which corresponds to Paul's 'Damascus road' or Augustine's 'Tolle Lege' is the experience at Caesarea Philippi which is recognized to be a watershed in St Mark's narrative. When the disciples were first recruited they were giving their allegiance to a young rabbi well versed in the Scriptures, with a remarkably light and authoritative touch. Like the rest of the people, they 'heard Him gladly'. Whilst their recruitment constituted a marked breach with the past, there was nothing otherwise exceptional about it. Many a rabbi gathered to himself a school of disciples (often twelve in number) who shared his life, helped to provide for his needs and listened to his teaching. Many a guru in our own day does the same.

The Gospel of Mark is perhaps best interpreted as a 'study in discipleship' (see 'Discipleship in Mark' in *Following Jesus* by Ernest Best, University of Sheffield, 1981). The instruction of the disciples takes two forms in the Gospel. There are examples of what we might call Our Lord's academic teaching on the nature of the Kingdom, followed by experiences of the powers of the Kingdom at work in the healing of bodies and minds. The disciples were not immune to the currents of thought in the Judaism of their day. They would be looking for a prophet, a teacher of righteousness, a Messiah who was to fulfil the hopes of Israel. And so discipleship for them meant a process of education by which they were weaned away from lurid or worldly estimates of a Messiah. The climax of this process came at Caesarea Philippi, where their progress in discipleship was tested with one blunt inescapable question.

And Jesus went on with his disciples, to the villages of Caesarea Philippi; and on the way he asked his disciples, 'Who do men say that I am?' And they told him, 'John the Baptist; and others say, Elijah; and others one of the prophets.' And he asked them, 'But who do you say that I am?' Peter answered him, 'You are the Christ.' And he charged them to tell no one about him. (Mark 8:27–30)

This affirmation was far from being the affirmation of a full-orbed faith in the pre-existence and deity of Christ. The word 'Christ' means 'the anointed one' and came in later Judaism to be associated with the Messiah. Peter is not therefore assenting to the Apostles Creed, which is a much later stage in the development of Christian thought; he is affirming what he can, and that on the basis of personal experience – he cannot but believe that this Jesus of Nazareth somehow is to be identified with the long-awaited Saviour of Israel. This faith was to be severely shaken in the coming events in Jerusalem but it was the moment in which Peter, and with him the other disciples, broke the false images which they had carried about with them and worshipped the one true representative of God on earth. So, the conversion of Peter corresponds in Mark's mind to the conversion of Paul, although it was not accompanied by any blinding light or any voice from Heaven. Behind Peter's conversion lies a long history of membership of the people of God, of hopes and aspirations and doubts and fears, and behind all that the loving providence of Almighty God bringing many sons to glory. St Matthew's version of the Caesarea incident makes the point – 'Blessed are you Simon Bar-Jona, for flesh and blood have not revealed this to you but my Father who is in Heaven' (16:17).

We are in a better position now to estimate the source of the faith by which Paul lived. It was a faith made articulate in the vision on the Damascus road which was the culmination of a long process of spiritual education back through his persecution of the church, his work as a rabbi, his education at the feet of Gamaliel in Jerusalem, his struggles with the engulfing Hellenism of his native city Tarsus, the faith of his fathers, his membership of the chosen people. The history of his faith ran back to Jacob his forefather and behind that to Abraham and the birth of the human race. He could have said, and indeed does say in a different form in the course of his letter writing, what Mark Kinzer, himself a Jewish Christian, says in the book *The Witness of the Jews to God* (The Handsel Press, 1982)

Indeed, faith in the Messiah has fulfilled my Judaism. To be more precise, it has brought me back to the God of Israel whom I abandoned in my youth. I was an assimilated Jew, independent, cynical, and unbelieving, yet hungry for knowledge and truth, and Yeshua revealed himself to me as the wisdom and the power of God. To be even more precise, faith in the Messiah has brought me forward to a new Judaism consummated in the death and resurrection of Yeshua and already bringing forth the first-fruits of the life of the age to come.

The sources of faith remain a mystery as those who have any experience of it will know, but it is a mystery with which we have to learn to co-operate as St Paul did and St Augustine did and the disciples and Mark Kinzer – and many other unsung heroes who through faith conquer kingdoms and enforce justice, escape the edge of the sword, win strength out of weakness, become mighty in war, put foreign armies to flight.

The whole of existence frightens me, from the smallest fly to the mystery of the Incarnation, everything is unintelligible to me, most of all myself; the whole of existence is poisoned in my sight, particularly myself. Great is my sorrow and without bounds; no man knows it, only God in heaven, and he will not console me; no man can console me, only God in heaven and he will not have mercy upon me.

Søhren Kierkegaard (Journal 1839)*

*From *A Kierkegaard Anthology*, ed. Robert Bretall, OUP, 1947.

4 FAITH AND FEAR

They were sitting in front of me in my study at Bishopthorpe having left their baby in the pram in the waiting room outside. They were rather tense. Had they come to see me about some marriage problem, some scandal in the parish, some crisis at work? Were they there to engage my support for some well-meaning charity? They wasted no time on preliminaries. They were there to ask me what I thought of the CND movement. For, so it appeared, they were enthusiastically attached to that cause and, as the husband himself admitted, they were preoccupied with it. It was on the menu for breakfast, lunch and tea; he bored his colleagues with it at work and drove his friends to distraction. Why, I asked, had this so suddenly come to dominate their minds? We, I said (appealing to my superior age), had been living with the possibility of nuclear war for over thirty years. What had happened to raise this spectre in their minds? They did not offer an answer, but the answer was obvious – it was the baby crying in the pram in the room next door. As someone else said within a few weeks of that interview, 'I do not want to see my children incinerated.' Suddenly – and it was comparatively sudden – the CND had recaptured the ground it had been steadily losing over the previous ten years, and many of its new supporters were young married people rearing their families, and for what purpose? they ask themselves. One little girl, when asked by her uncle what she was going to do when she grew up, began her reply with – 'If I grow up . . .' That interview suggested to me how far my own senses had been dulled to the threat of a nuclear holocaust with which men and women of my generation had been living ever since the Second World War, and I felt myself ill-equipped to deal with the lacerating fears of this young couple beside me. I subsequently wrote to them a more considered reply and I quote part of it now:

Nuclear war is a horrendous possibility and you are right to try to cause people to take it seriously, but it is not the only horrendous possibility as I think Ronald Higgins' book *The Seventh Enemy* will show. 'Dread' may well attach to nuclear warfare as the ultimate horror but dread is an innate constituent of the human condition and will attach itself to anything. The Old Testament abounds in illustrations of dread as it was experienced by, for example, the patriarchs, by the prophets and in the New Testament ultimately by our Lord Himself. It proceeds from a fundamental insecurity on the earth which needs to be faced, not exclusively in the light of some distant historical possibility but in the light of our situation here and now. The dread of death and annihilation is inescapable – inescapable except insofar as we can assent to that great utterance in the Bible – 'The Eternal God is our refuge and underneath me are the everlasting arms.' I would have to say that this is my only resource for everyday living. (1 May 1980)

This interview was the beginning of a series of engagements, by public meetings and by correspondence, prompted by that fear which I encountered that afternoon in my own study. On one such occasion I was asked by a local Council of Churches in North Yorkshire to speak on 'The Christian response to the nuclear threat'. Having learnt by then the hard way that I was not equipped to speak on the subject without support, I took with me two nuclear physicists, both of whom had at one time or another in their careers been involved in the preparations for and precautions against nuclear war. They spoke on the technical aspects of it and spoke with chilling confidence of the likely effects of even a small nuclear strike upon the cities of this land. Their speeches were all the more effective for the cool, detached attitude we have come to expect from scientific men, but underneath was a passionate concern for the future of mankind on the earth.

I found myself in a situation which must be familiar to anyone who has to do a lot of public speaking. A kind of chill spread through the audience as the disquisition proceeded and I began to turn over in my mind rather despairingly the kind of remarks I had prepared myself to make when the nuclear physicists sat down. I recalled a story by Cecil

Hallack in her book *The Happiness of Father Happe* about a house-party which Father Happe was attending with a view to celebrating Mass the following morning. The evening promised the usual small talk, the careless ribaldry and evanescent conversation. The door opened and a pale, very flustered member of the domestic staff broke in to say in a loud whisper to the host – 'She's dead'. It was as if, Cecily Hallack said, a shiver passed through the members of the house-party as those happy pagans looked into the darkness into which all of them would one day disappear. But these 300 people attending a meeting in a North Yorkshire town were, for the most part, Christians, not 'happy pagans'. What was I to say to them, now firmly gripped by the fear of those things which could one day be happening upon the earth?

The opening of my own speech was conventional enough. Yes, Christians ought to be associating themselves with any political efforts to reduce or abolish nuclear arms. Yes, Christians could, and perhaps should, take an interest in such civil defence measures as proved to be feasible. Yes, we should be striving to reduce tension wherever it was found. Peace was indivisible – a seemingly minor conflict this week could lead to a nuclear devastation the next. But when all that was said, it was far from being a distinctively Christian response. The uncomfortable fact was that we should have to live forever with the threat of nuclear war. No disarmament programme, however vigorously pursued by the great powers, no system of surveillance, however comprehensive, would ever wholly exclude the possibility that some minor world power, or even some terrorist group, could acquire a nuclear capability and devastate the earth. So we were going to have to live with the nuclear threat forever, and the Christian's problem was how to cope with the fear, not just with the threat.

I have had occasion to rehearse those arguments several times since that evening in the school assembly hall in North Yorkshire. I have become increasingly aware of that spectre of nuclear war which can haunt the seemingly carefree party, or blight the hopes of a young couple as they stand at the font for the baptism of their child, or destroy the will to live of a university student with everything, apparently, to live for, or demoralize the lonely viewer in front of his television set. What are we to do with this fear, which can undermine the health of individuals and put at risk whole societies? In

1978 Miss Barbara Tuchman wrote a book called *A Distant Mirror* (Macmillan, 1979). It was a history of the fourteenth century, called 'A Distant Mirror' because, as Miss Tuchman perceived it, it was a calamitous century not unlike the century in which we ourselves are living. It was a century in which the structures of society simply fell apart. This is what she says about the Black Death, in some ways so analogous to the threat of nuclear war:

Lawlessness and debauchery accompanied the plague as they had during the great plague of Athens of 430 B.C., when according to Thucydides, men grew bold in the indulgence of pleasure: 'For seeing how the rich died in a moment and those who had nothing immediately inherited their property, they reflected that life and riches were alike transitory and they resolved to enjoy themselves while they could.' Human behaviour is timeless. When St John had his vision of plague in Revelation, he knew from some experience or race memory that those who survived 'repented not of the work of their hands ... Neither repented they of their murders, nor of their sorceries, nor of their fornication, nor of their thefts.'

The phantom enemy had no name. Called the Black Death only in later recurrences, it was known during the first epidemic simply as the Pestilence or Great Mortality. Reports from the East, swollen by fearful imaginings, told of strange tempests and 'sheets of fire' mingled with huge hailstones that 'slew almost all,' or a 'vast rain of fire' that burned up men, beasts, stones, trees, villages, and cities. In another version, 'foul blasts of wind' from the fires carried the infection to Europe 'and now as some suspect it cometh round the seacoast'. Accurate observation in this case could not make the mental jump to ships and rats because no idea of animal- or insect-borne contagion existed.

The earthquake was blamed for releasing sulfurous and foul fumes from the earth's interior, or as evidence of a titanic struggle of planets and oceans causing waters to rise and vaporize until fish died in masses and corrupted the air. All these explanations had in common a factor of poisoned air, of miasmas and thick, stinking mists traced to every kind of natural or imagined agency from stagnant lakes to malign conjunction of the planets, from the hand of the Evil One to the wrath of God. Medical thinking, trapped in the theory of astral influences, stressed air as the communicator of disease, ignoring sanitation or visible carriers. The existence of two carriers confused the trail, the more so because the flea could live and travel independently of the rat for as long as a month and, if infected by the particularly virulent septicemic form of the bacillus, could infect humans without reinfecting itself from the rat. The simultaneous presence of the pneumonic form of the disease, which was indeed communicated through the air, blurred the problem further.

The mystery of the contagion was 'the most terrible of all the terrors', as an anonymous Flemish cleric in Avignon wrote to a correspondent in Bruges.

'The most terrible of all the terrors,' many an anonymous cleric today might say of the prospect of nuclear war. But observe that the mortality rates, huge though they were, were in the end less significant than the mortal fear which gripped whole populations, leading not only to 'lawlessness and debauchery' but to violent crimes against society, witch-hunts, pogroms against the Jews, and the collapse of a world-view which proved no match for the fearful events in which men and women were involved. It left a gaping wound in the world which has never wholly been healed since. And one day, as Albert Camus said in his novel *The Plague* (Penguin, 1948) it could happen again:

And, indeed, as he listened to the cries of joy rising from the town, Rieux remembered that such joy is always imperilled. He knew what those jubilant crowds did not know but could have learned from books: that the plague bacillus never dies or disappears for good; that it can lie dormant for years and years in furniture and linen-chests; that it bides its time in bedrooms, cellars, trunks, and bookshelves; and that perhaps the day would come when, for the bane and the enlightening of men, it roused up its rats again and sent them forth to die in a happy city.

I can well understand the agitation of the young couple who came to see me about the threat of nuclear war. But there is no way the threat can be removed from mankind for the rest of time. The rats can always come again to die in a happy city, bringing death and destruction with them. What is the Christian response, therefore, not only to the threat but to the fear? World society might well be undermined by the fear long before the mushroom cloud appears over its cities, and preoccupation with this particular peril may well blind our eyes to the subtler dangers which beset us. Ronald Higgins' book *The Seventh Enemy* (Hodder & Stoughton, 1978) does indeed include the nuclear threat but includes six other potent threats to the survival of mankind into the twenty-first century. The same point is made in a different way by Professor J. M. Roberts (*Pelican History of the World*, Penguin, 1980) in the following paragraph:

Some doubts which have recently arisen about our civilization agree that it is supremely good at creating material improvement, but note that wealth in itself does not remove all man's dissatisfactions and may actually irritate some of them more acutely. Pollution, the oppressive anonymity of crowded cities and the nervous stress and strain of modern work conditions do much to erase satisfaction with a mere increase of material goods. Things have come to a pretty pass in one of the most beautiful cities in the world when, as we now discover, the noise level in the Place de l'Opera is greater than that at the Niagara Falls, and the Seine is found to carry more sewer water than its natural flow. Scale has become a problem in its own right, too, as well as creating others. Problems made bigger in modern cities may even have grown to the point at which they are insoluble. Still greater misgivings are felt about the threat of over-population and the reality of increasing pressure on diminishing energy resources – with the result, perhaps, that competition for them must grow more intense and the world in consequence more politically unstable. In any case, energy and material resources are now so wastefully and inequitably employed that a new version of the Malthusian peril seems likely. Whereas we have by no means reached the end (or anything like it) of our capacity to produce food, it is far more likely that other things will run out before food does so, whatever may be the hardships experienced from time to time in specific places. Certainly there would at once be an impossible situation if every nation in the world sought to consume goods other than foods at the level of the developed countries today.

This is from the last chapter, entitled 'In the Light of History', and it is perhaps significant that it does not allude to the nuclear threat, nor does the phrase occur in the index. Does that betray an unawareness of the issue (which scarcely seems likely); is it not rather due to the kind of sense of proportion which a historian may acquire as he views the future 'in the light of history'? The Christian response to the nuclear threat should certainly exhibit that sense of proportion, not only in the light of history but in the light of eternity. But the fear of what is happening on the earth does not arise only from the nuclear threat, nor is it peculiar to this generation. There is, at the heart of every man, a sense of dread which will indeed fasten onto events or situations feared, but is at its most potent when it is unrecognized and unaccepted, deep in the psyche of the human being.

In a sermon to Rotary International in York Minster early in 1980 I permitted myself an unfortunate aside which, as always, was intended as an illustration, but in the minds of the reporters present became the subject of the whole sermon. I happened to comment upon a news programme in the previous week which, as I remember it, included riots in the streets of Germany, a confrontation with pickets outside one of our English factories, a road disaster of some magnitude on the M62, and the report of a particularly gruesome murder case. And then the weather man came on, took off his sunshine symbols, smothered the whole country with clouds, and uttered a dire warning of the appalling weather which awaited us on the following day. Might it not be wiser, I said, for the news editors to seek a better balance of news which included at least one item per evening of good news. I was pursued for interviews with the Press that evening, rewarded with a splendid cartoon by Giles the following morning, and almost at once plunged into controversy with the news department of the BBC. My comment was not intended as a criticism of the BBC, although it was inevitably regarded as such. It was an attempt to expose the risks we face in society when we touch the tender nerve of fear. One of the reporters who interviewed me that evening admitted that he often sat in his

chair in front of the television screen at news time with his
ears pinned back waiting for the next horror. This was no
elderly valetudinarian who was interviewing me, but a hearty
young man at home in a Rugby scrum, who as a reporter
was constantly on the scene in the presence of death, violence
and conflict. The correspondence with the BBC was carried
on in a most friendly spirit, but was brought to a grinding
halt by the suggestion that every applicant for a post in the
news-room should be asked whether he had read Kierkegaard's *Concept of Dread*. That was indeed a somewhat flashy
remark on my part, but there is truth in it. Kierkegaard said
of himself – 'everything frightens me, life itself frightens me'.
What then is the Christian response to the universal experience of dread, to whatever passing fear it may be attached?

A striking feature of St Mark's Gospel, although not
confined to that gospel, is the verbal association of two words,
'fear' and 'faith'. The section 4:35 to 5:43 is the account
of the disciples' encounter with a series of mounting crises,
accompanied by mounting acts of power by our Lord. They
experienced first of all the storm on the lake; they are rebuked
by Christ for the panic which overtook them – 'Why are you
afraid? Have you no faith?' Having been delivered safely to
the other side of the lake they encounter a dangerous lunatic
no man could manage. He was healed by Christ. Then follows
the healing of the woman who had had an issue of blood for
twelve years, who overcame her fear of publicity in order to
touch the hem of Christ's garment and was rewarded with
the saying – 'your faith has made you whole'. After the delay
occasioned by that incident, Jesus and His disciples arrived
at the house of the Ruler of the Synagogue whose daughter
was dead. He said to the Ruler, 'Do not fear, only believe,'
and the daughter was raised from the dead.

This passage is so familiar that we sometimes overlook one
striking aspect of it and that is the unvarying contrast which
is made by the evangelist between faith and fear, when we
might have expected contrast between faith and unbelief. St
Mark is simply making the point, which was presumably
made to those first disciples, that the only remedy for fear is
faith, not as a series of dogmatic assertions but as a confident
affirmation of the loving providence of God. The miracles of
the New Testament, as of the Old Testament, are signs of
God's presence in the most intransigent and fearful circum-

stances in which we may be involved. 'Fear not, little flock,' our Lord said to His disciples, 'for it is the Father's good pleasure to give you the kingdom' (Luke 12:32). It was that faith which carried the apostles through many a fearful encounter and through many a dark place in an unfailingly hostile world. In Bunyan's *Pilgrim's Progress* the porter at the lodge 'whose name was Watchful, replied to the Pilgrim saying – fear not the lions for they are chained'.

I end with a personal anecdote which may help to earth the discussion in this chapter in the soil of everyday life. From very near the beginning of my own ministry I have been aware of tension and have over the years taken what I suppose to be sensible precautions against it by reserving time for rest and positive relaxation. But I was aware of living uncomfortably near the edge of my own endurance and have indeed toppled over it once or twice. I asked my doctor on one occasion what was the cause of tension. He replied instantly, and with what I took to be a meaningful look, 'There is only one cause of tension and that is fear.' For every one person who is afraid of nuclear war there are thousands who are afraid. But of what? – illness, failure, marital breakdown, death. It is precisely because it is so difficult to identify the cause of fear that it is so potent. As the Psalmist said of himself – 'He was afraid where no fear was.' The dosage of tranquillizers consumed in the Western nations is evidence of a prevailing fear which only faith (not tranquillizers) can cure. It is he who sees beyond the veil who knows that the lions are chained, that he cannot drift outside God's love and care. Only so can we be delivered from the fear which the poet expresses:

Sometimes I have a sin of fear
that when I have spun my last thread
I shall perish on the shore.

NO SCAR?

Hast thou no scar?
No hidden scar on foot, or side, or hand?
I hear thee sung as mighty in the land,
I hear them hail thy bright ascendant star,
Hast thou no scar?

Hast thou no wound?
Yet I was wounded by the archers, spent,
Leaned Me against a tree to die; and rent
By ravening beasts that compassed Me, I
    swooned:
Hast thou no wound?

No wound? no scar?
Yet, as the Master shall the servant be,
And pierced are the feet that follow Me;
But thine are whole: can he have followed far
Who has nor wound nor scar?

Amy Carmichael – 1936*
(*Toward Jerusalem*, SPCK, 1944)

*Taken from copyright material used by permission of SPCK and the Christian Literature Crusade, Fort Washington, Pa. 19034.

5 FAITH AND SUFFERING

The New Testament is rich in the language of suffering, variously translated in the English versions as afflictions, distresses, straits, trials, perils, anguish. This is hardly surprising in a world which was without a National Health Service, without anaesthetics, welfare benefits, unemployment pay, in a world which made no provision for the old or the dying, a world which could be ravaged by locusts one year and by marauding armies the next, a world in which rough justice prevailed and hideous punishments were meted out. The Greek words which stand behind our translation are often interchangeable and, where they are not, they merely suggest refinements of the universal experience of suffering.

Our sufferings in the twentieth century are of a different kind, perhaps calling for a different word, but they are every bit as deadly – and what makes them particularly deadly is the perplexity of heart and mind which accompanies them. The man stricken down in the prime of life cannot but ask the question – why? The woman with a young family who undergoes a routine check and discovers the awful truth, is not only afraid, she is bewildered. And even where some of us have been lucky enough to escape such afflictions we cannot but be aware of the sheer weight of suffering which bears humanity down. It is not just a question, it is the question, with which mankind has struggled from the beginning of time. This is how a twentieth-century man* puts it:

Brief and powerless is man's life; on him and all his race the slow, sure doom falls pitiless and dark. Blind to good and evil, reckless of destruction, omnipotent matter rolls on its relentless way; for man, condemned today to lose

*Bertrand Russell, in *Why I Am Not a Christian*, National Secular Society.

his dearest, tomorrow himself to pass through the gate of darkness, it remains only to cherish, ere yet the blow fall, the lofty thoughts that ennoble his little day; disdaining the coward terrors of the slave of Fate, to worship at the shrine that his own hands have built; undismayed by the empire of chance, to preserve a mind free from the wanton tyranny that rules his outward life; proudly defiant of the irresistible forces that tolerate, for a moment, his knowledge and his condemnation, to sustain, alone, a weary but unyielding Atlas, the world that his own ideals have fashioned despite the trampling march of unconscious power.

Bertrand Russell, as he acknowledges, was not a Christian, and as becomes an eminent mathematician, he had logic on his side. This is how the world looks to any sensitive man who dares to look at it – 'Blind to good and evil, reckless of destruction, omnipotent matter rolls on its relentless way.' But then, many a Christian is in no better case. He professes to believe in the love of God but in his heart there is a dead weight of despair, even when he is outwardly strong, healthy and fortunate. As someone vouchsafed to me in a remark recently – 'I can believe in a loving providence for myself as I look back over my life but I find it difficult to see it in the total suffering of mankind.' If, therefore, there is any human condition which demands faith to become bearable it is this one – the experience of inevitable, universal suffering, taking different forms in differing ages and in differing societies, but inescapable.

Long before Bertrand Russell addressed his intellect to this problem, great minds had grappled with it, seeking not necessarily relief from their sufferings but some explanation for them. Those readers familiar with the Bible will expect me to refer at once to the Book of Job. But that is not so obvious a source as it might seem. The book is not primarily about the problem of suffering but about the difference between an academic and an experiential view of life. Put another way, Job finds the intellectual structures of his day unable to bear the weight of his experience and rails violently against them. Nevertheless the occasion of this discourse was the experience of suffering – the writer's own no doubt, but in the form of a familiar story about the wise man of the East,

Job famous for his patience. His 'patience' was tested not so much by his sufferings, which were real enough and are described at length in the first two chapters, but by the kindly but maddening explanations which the so-called 'comforters' offered him. 'It must be the will of God,' they said; 'It must be good for him,' or 'He must have been, contrary to all the evidence, a wicked man who is now paying the price of his wickedness.' Thus they tormented him, as he sat on the heap outside the city, with a variety of banal explanations which he fiercely rejects. 'Miserable comforters are you all,' he says, and cries out in agony, 'O that I knew where I might find him, that I might come even to his seat. I would lay my case before him and fill my mouth with arguments' (Job 23:3–4). Observe that in the very depths of despair he clings to a residuum of faith which against all the evidence presupposes the existence of One who hears and answers prayer. The book offers no explanations of suffering other than ones already discredited, but culminates in a transcending vision of the Living God in whose presence no explanations are necessary.

Then Job answered the Lord:
'I know that thou canst do all things,
   and that no purpose of thine can be thwarted.
'Who is this that hides counsel without knowledge?'
Therefore I have uttered what I did not understand,
   things too wonderful for me, which I did not know.
'Hear, and I will speak;
   I will question you, and you declare to me.'
I had heard of thee by the hearing of the ear,
   but now my eye sees thee;
therefore I despise myself,
   and repent in dust and ashes.

(Job 42:1–6)

Other explanations are on offer in the Old Testament but none that would satisfy Bertrand Russell's quest for reassurance. The arguments offered by the comforters in the Book of Job are rehearsed in different ways elsewhere. For example, the sufferings of Israel in the wilderness are regarded as the means by which God prepares them for the Promised Land. The writer of 1 and 2 Samuel and 1 and 2 Kings (the former prophets) seeks to account for the fall of Jerusalem, the destruction of the Temple and the demise of the monarchy by rehearsing the long history of Israel's apostasy. But the frankest observer of human life represented in the Old Testament comes up with a conclusion not dissimilar to that of Bertrand Russell.

Again I saw all the oppressions that are practised under the sun. And behold, the tears of the oppressed, and they had no one to comfort them! On the side of their oppressors there was power, and there was no one to comfort them. And I thought the dead who are already dead more fortunate than the living who are still alive; but better than both is he who has not yet been, and has not seen the evil deeds that are done under the sun. (Ecclesiastes 4:1–3)

When St Paul said that he was living by faith in the Son of God who loved him and gave himself for him, he was living by faith in the world of the first century, without the medical and welfare facilities which we take for granted. His letters abound with a variety of words for suffering. You can demonstrate it for yourself by going through the Epistles and underlining any word which conveys the meaning of suffering in one form or another. I think I can promise that you will find several hundreds. But if you want a shorter, less demanding exercise, then look for one such word, 'weak' or 'weakness' in one particular part of his correspondence – the letters to the Corinthians. This noun or the adjective appear twenty-two times. The reader may be surprised to find the term 'weakness' associated so strongly with an Apostle one might have supposed was remarkable for his strength – a man of indomitable will, heroic endurance and superb intellect. Yet it is the sense of weakness rather than of strength which dominates St Paul's inner life. Certainly his sufferings were very great by any standards, ancient or modern. He often recites them, and here is a variation on the theme in 2 Corinthians (11:23–7):

... far greater labours, far more imprisonments, with countless beatings, and often near death. Five times I have received at the hands of the Jews the forty lashes less one. Three times I have been beaten with rods; once I was stoned. Three times I have been shipwrecked; a night and a day I have been adrift at sea; on frequent journeys, in danger from rivers, danger from robbers, danger from my own people, danger from Gentiles, danger in the city, danger in the wilderness, danger at sea, danger from false brethren; in toil and hardship, through many a sleepless night, in hunger and thirst, often without food, in cold and exposure.

But these physical afflictions were as nothing in St Paul's mind compared with his inner afflictions arising from what he called 'the care of all the Churches'.

In that phrase 'the care of all the Churches' lies a whole world of meaning which would not be obvious to the casual reader. His work as an evangelist, to which he had been called, so he supposed, by God Himself, provoked intense opposition not only from his erstwhile colleagues, the leaders of Israel, but from people who came to be known later as 'Gnostics' who confronted his simple Gospel and sought to undermine it with a very sophisticated form of religion which named the name of Christ but was far removed from the apostolic testimony to Him. Moreover, even without those 'aids' from outside, the churches showed a chronic tendency to divide within themselves, some following Peter, some following Apollos and some following Paul. Even in the earliest days of the Christian Church Paul found himself cast in the role of an ecumenist; and even in his own entourage were those who were ultimately to desert him. Demas for example, or Mark, the author of the second Gospel. Why suffer perils in the deep, hunger and thirst, encounters with robbers if the flimsy structures of the Church he had created proved so vulnerable?

But even deeper still in the innermost sanctuary of St Paul's life there must have remained the lurking anxiety about his own role and status in the providence of God. Under the impetus of that striking revelation on the road to Damascus he went out to conquer the world for Christ, but the revelation did not solve all his problems. He had parted company with sincere religious men who had once been his colleagues or his mentors. He had put himself outside the sacred company of the chosen people. He was accused of being an apostate himself from the religion of his fathers. And yet at the same time he found himself ill at ease with the so-called 'pillars of the Church', at odds with them on many important matters, and an object of suspicion amongst those with whom, at enormous sacrifice, he had thrown in his lot. It was a harsh world in which St Paul lived and it was a harsh inner life he had somehow to come to terms with. But how was he to come to terms with this persistent experience of suffering?

There is no evidence that he was satisfied, or could be satisfied, with the peremptory solutions of the Jewish tradition, against which Job had inveighed. He could live probably with the suggestion that his sufferings were a form of probation for the future life, but he never showed any consciousness of the possibility that his sufferings were the consequence of personal sin. But he cannot be content either with the studied agnosticism of the writer of the book of Ecclesiastes. His own religious background, both Jewish and Christian, prohibited the kind of despair which is reflected in Bertrand Russell's view of life. But even the Old Testament was not without its hints, and, rabbi as he was, he would not have been the man to miss them. He might, for example, have pondered the strange experience of the so-called 'suffering servant' whose dim outlines are to be observed in the second section of the prophecy of Isaiah – the one who 'had no form or comeliness . . . and no beauty that we should desire him . . . despised and rejected of men, a man of sorrows and acquainted with grief'. The author of that passage had known about seemingly meaningless suffering but rises above it with this astonishing assertion of faith:

Surely he has borne our griefs
    and carried our sorrows;
yet we esteemed him stricken,
    smitten by God, and afflicted.
But he was wounded for our transgressions,
    he was bruised for our iniquities;
upon him was the chastisement that made us whole,
    and with his stripes we are healed.
All we like sheep have gone astray;
    we have turned every one to his own way;
and the Lord has laid on him
    the iniquity of us all.

(Isaiah 53:4–6)

But even if St Paul had not applied these words to himself he would certainly have known of their application to the Christ who had called him on the Damascus road, for he too had been a man of sorrows and acquainted with grief, and upon him, so the early Christians believed, had been laid the iniquity of us all.

The story of the suffering servant does not stand entirely on its own in the Old Testament, insofar as the theme of strength out of weakness, victory out of defeat, is made familiar in the lives of many of God's servants. Moses had resisted the call of God on the basis of his own inadequacy and weakness ('I am a poor speaker'). Jacob was far less well equipped by nature and by temperament than Esau his brother, but it was he who was to be the father of the people. David was a mere boy when he confronted Goliath and slew him with a sling and a sword. But perhaps the most striking variation on this theme is the saga connected with the name of Samson. Even when allowance is made for some pious exaggeration, Samson was a mighty warrior and a man of seemingly super-human strength. But then, in thrall to the Philistine woman he had betrayed the secret of his strength and was seized by his enemies and imprisoned eyeless in Gaza. Here is the matchless account of his death in Judges (16:23–30):

Now the lords of the Philistines gathered to offer a great sacrifice to Dagon their god, and to rejoice; for they said, 'Our god has given Samson our enemy into our hand.' And when the people saw him, they praised their god; for they said, 'Our god has given our enemy into our hand, the ravager of our country, who has slain many of us.' And when their hearts were merry, they said, 'Call Samson, that he may make sport for us.' So they called Samson out of the prison, and he made sport before them. They made him stand between the pillars; and Samson said to the lad who held him by the hand, 'Let me feel the pillars on which the house rests, that I may lean against them.' Now the house was full of men and women; all the lords of the Philistines were there, and on the roof there were about three thousand men and women, who looked on while Samson made sport.

Then Samson called to the Lord and said, 'O Lord God,

remember me, I pray thee, and strengthen me, I pray thee, only this once, O God, that I may be avenged upon the Philistines for one of my two eyes.' And Samson grasped the two middle pillars upon which the house rested, and he leaned his weight upon them, his right hand on the one and his left hand on the other. And Samson said, 'Let me die with the Philistines.' Then he bowed with all his might; and the house fell upon the lords and upon all the people that were in it. So the dead whom he slew at his death were more than those whom he had slain during his life.

It is difficult to read this story without hearing echoes of some of Paul's characteristic expressions. 'God has chosen the weak things of the world to confound the strong' – 'When I am weak then am I strong' – 'The weakness of God is stronger than men' – 'My strength is made perfect in weakness'.

Bertrand Russell was right. There is no explanation for suffering which can satisfy the thinking man – 'brief and powerless is man's life; on him and all his race the slow sure doom falls pitiless and dark'. But within that darkness there are sufficient glimpses for the man of faith to enjoy some reassurance. Paul was such a man of faith.

In the end St Paul's inner life is probably of more consequence in the life of the Spirit than even his most spectacular triumphs in Philippi and Ephesus and Athens and Rome. For circumstances drove him to consider more deeply than most the nature and meaning of that suffering which underlay the surface of his active life. In the personal account, thrice repeated, of his conversion experience he recalls a blinding vision and a vocation to be an apostle to the Gentiles. But privately, to Ananias, that humble disciple of Christ in Damascus, was revealed another aspect of that great ministry. The Lord said to Ananias, 'Paul is a chosen vessel unto me, to bear my name before the Gentiles and kings, and the children of Israel; for I will show him how great things he must suffer for my name's sake' (Acts 9:15–16). That part of the message Ananias did not convey to the man lying blind and helpless in the street called Straight. It was a lesson Paul was going to have to learn for himself. And learn it he did, and the evidences for his understanding of suffering are present in the Epistles. He bore in his own body the marks of the Lord Jesus (Galatians 6:17), he experienced the fellowship of Christ's sufferings (Philippians 3:10), he was 'crucified with Christ' (Galatians 2:20) and he even went so far as to give expression to a conviction which has troubled dogmatic theologians ever since, he 'filled up the sufferings of Christ' (Colossians 1:24). So he was the suffering servant of the Christ, who was the suffering servant of God. These sufferings of body and mind and spirit were not just accidents of time to be endured and, if possible, dismissed; they were a sharing in the redemptive work of Christ; they were, by a curious 'exchange' the means by which others found life and health. This is why he is able to say:

> . . . a thorn was given me in the flesh, a messenger of Satan, to harass me, to keep me from being too elated. Three times I besought the Lord about this, that it should leave me; but he said to me, 'My grace is sufficient for you, for my power is made perfect in weakness.' I will all the more gladly boast of my weaknesses, that the power of Christ may rest upon me. For the sake of Christ, then, I am content with weaknesses, insults, hardships, persecutions, and calamities; for when I am weak, then I am strong. (2 Corinthians 12:7–10)

This is an astonishing and daring insight into the relationship between faith and suffering, and is only equalled in my own experience by the words of Kierkegaard:

> The birds in the branches, the lilies in the field, the deer in the forest, the fish in the sea, countless hosts of happy men exultantly proclaim – God is love. But beneath all these sopranos, supporting them, as it were, with the bass part, is audible the *de profundis* which issues from those who are sacrificed: God is love.

THE GREAT DUST-HEAP

Sometimes it seems pure natural to trust,
And trust right largely, grandly, infinitely,
Daring the splendour of the giver's part;
At other times, the whole earth is but dust,
The sky is dust, yea, dust the human heart;
Then art thou nowhere, there is no room for
  thee
In the great dust-heap of eternity.

George MacDonald (*Diary of an Old Soul*,
        Arthur C. Fifield, 1905)

Life is doubt and faith without doubt is
  nothing but death.

Miguel de Unamuno (1907)

6   FAITH AND DOUBT

Doubt is an aspect of suffering, experienced at various levels of human consciousness. Look at the football manager in his little box on the touch-line, smoking incessantly or chewing gum, moving restlessly on his bench, tormented with doubt as to whether he can safely launch his substitute at this stage in the game or whether he ought to withhold him for fear of an injury to one of his players. Spare a thought for the navigator in a less-computerized age as he tries to answer the pilot's question – 'X gallons of petrol. Do we go on, or turn back?' Or consider the surgeon with a life in his hands, as he faces a situation not previously revealed by the X-ray. Many a young school-leaver will know the pain of trying to reach a conclusion about his next step. I myself have stood in an agony of indecision on wholly inconsequential matters – whether to catch this train or the next one, whether to buy this suit or a different one. Every assistant in a shoe shop will at some time or other encounter the chronic doubter who ends up with twenty shoes scattered on the floor and goes out of the shop empty-handed. The word 'doubt', like the word 'faith' is not just a religious concept; it is the painful experience of us all.

When we turn from these relatively trivial illustrations to the Bible itself we are confronted with a difficult, but ultimately instructive problem. In the English versions of the New Testament, for example, the word for 'doubt' or 'doubter' is relatively uncommon but the language often reflects an experience of doubt even when it is expressed in other forms. The position is much the same in the original Greek, in which a number of words are pressed into service. The obvious word is 'apistos', which is a privative form and suggests the opposite of faith. But elsewhere, experience of doubt is expressed in a bewildering variety of words, suggesting double-mindedness, hesitation, questioning, indecision, instability. The basic thought suggested by the form of all these words is division. The football manager on the bench is struggling with a divided mind – and so is the surgeon and the navigator and the school-leaver. So doubt does not exclude faith; it can live alongside it, and both are perfectly expressed in an incident from St Matthew's Gospel:

> And Peter answered him, 'Lord, if it is you, bid me come to you on the water.' He said, 'Come.' So Peter got out of the boat and walked on the water and came to Jesus; but when he saw the wind, he was afraid, and beginning to sink he cried out, 'Lord, save me.' Jesus immediately reached out his hand and caught him, saying to him, 'O man of little faith, why did you doubt?' And when they got into the boat, the wind ceased. And those in the boat worshipped him, saying, 'Truly you are the Son of God.' (14:28–33)

This is perhaps the classic example in the New Testament of the human dilemma. Peter had faith enough to step out onto the water, and few of us could have emulated him, but doubt overtook him when he saw the wind and the waves. The incident issues in, as you will see, an almost formal affirmation of faith in Christ as the Messiah. This conjunction of doubt and faith is to be found almost everywhere in the Scriptures, both Old and New.

Insofar as we can derive little certainty from a study of the words themselves, we shall have to turn to what we must regard as familiar ways of expressing doubt in the most generalized sense of that term. What then are the doubts which assail the man who might wish to believe? For simplicity's sake I shall be confining my comments for the moment to doubts regarding the Christian faith, although they would no doubt have their parallels in every religion of the world.

There is a form of doubt which is little more than lack of conviction regarding certain religious doctrines or opinions, and these will be found as readily within the Christian Church as they will be found outside it. Such doubts were amply illustrated in the BBC programme in 1981 called 'Priestland's Progress', and in the letters (27,000 of them) by which listeners responded to the programme. For many of them

their doubts were no more than perfectly reasonable hesita-
tions about the dogma of the Church as they understood
them. So apparently the doctrine of the atonement was a
frequent stumbling block, and the doctrine of the Trinity was
a frequent occasion of confusion. The familiar forms in which
belief in the after-life are often expressed came in for heavy
criticism. And at a lower level altogether, the primacy and
the infallibility of the Pope was a fruitful occasion of doubt.
Gerald Priestland's reaction to this particular phase in his
programme is an expression of his own mind on the matter
as it had been influenced by his own 'progress':

I think, myself, that the infallibility of church assemblies
is as dubious as the infallibility of popes. Truth is not
necessarily ascertained by majority vote, and not more than
a fragment of the truth about God will ever be known by
any means. The best we can do is to acknowledge as wide
a Church as we possibly can (inevitably it will be suborgan-
ised into churches) and to maintain open dialogue within
it, neither seeking to compel others to accept our convictions nor rejecting theirs as mad. Some will press forward
down paths that lead nowhere; others will hang back and
refuse to move at all; from time to time, as in the past, the
whole body will get stuck in a confused mêlée; and at others
it will assume a unity and discipline that will carry it
forward in impressive style. But it has been on the road for
almost two thousand years, and I think it is not for any
individual of seventy years' span to usurp the role of the
Holy Spirit by presuming to say where it should go.*

On the whole I find myself in agreement with Gerald Priestland. Doubts of this kind are indeed obstacles to faith, as the
programme revealed, but they are not of the first order of
importance. The truth is always larger than the formulas by
which we seek to express it. A religious experience can never
be encapsulated within a doctrine, however useful that
doctrine may be in expressing a kind of common mind. Creeds
and confessions have no doubt played their part in guarding
the faithful against error but they are not necessarily in themselves powerful agents for the conviction of those who are not

*G. Priestland, *Priestland's Progress*, BBC Publications, 1982.

amongst the faithful. They are the products of centuries of history, they illustrate the social and intellectual convictions of the day, they were often the product of divisions in the Church which were due at least as much to political conflict as to intellectual argument. Indeed, as Gerald Priestland says, they are not infallible and their authors would never have supposed them to be so. They correspond to some dimly felt reality, but they are not necessarily the reality itself.

There are doubts, however, which penetrate much more closely to the heart of the matter and I am surprised to find how little currency they achieved in 'Priestland's Progress' and in the reactions to it. There are doubts indeed which imperil not simply the formulas of religion but the whole basis on which that religion is built. I refer to the great historical events associated with the life and times of Jesus of Nazareth. The record of these events is largely contained in the documents which subsequently achieved authority in the Church at large – namely, the New Testament and pre-eminently the Gospels themselves. The student of any ancient literature will know that any ancient document will itself have been subject to a process of adaptation, change and development. This is generally recognized to be true of the Old Testament documents, and, although over a shorter time range, must be true of the Gospels themselves.

Amongst the evangelists St Mark is the only one who can lay claim to any personal acquaintance with the people associated with the life and times of Jesus of Nazareth. The earliest known statements about the origins of the Gospel of St Mark are in a fragment from Papias, a second century writer, quoted by Eusebius:

'This also the presbyter used to say: Mark indeed, who became the interpreter of Peter, wrote accurately, as far as he remembered them, the things said or done by the Lord, but not however in order. For he had neither heard the Lord nor been His personal follower, but at a later stage, as I said, he had followed Peter, who used to adapt the teachings to the needs of his hearers, but not as though he were drawing up a connected account of the oracles of the Lord: so that Mark committed no error in writing certain matters just as he remembered them. For he had one object only in view, viz. to leave out nothing of the things which he had heard, and to include no false statement among them.' (Quoted in A. E. J. Rawlinson, The Gospel According to St Mark (Westminster Commentaries), Methuen, 6th edn 1947.)

Once it is recognized that the Gospels according to Matthew and Luke are derivative from Mark and that the fourth Gospel stands in a different category altogether, it will be seen upon how small a base the other literature of the New Testament and theological structure of the Church rest. Anyone, therefore, may be forgiven doubt on this score and many students of theology will themselves have had to wrestle with their newly acquired knowledge. But this is the kind of doubt which cannot be resolved; it is unlikely that there are any further documentary sources waiting to be uncovered in some ancient genizzah or other. St Mark's Gospel is all we have and all we are ever likely to have and we stand, therefore, unaided before a decision which has to be made.

I say 'unaided' but there are of course hints, allusions, insights, elsewhere in the New Testament literature which testifies to the confidence of the early Church in this early document. Whatever our view of it may be it remains, for good or ill, the most important document in the history of the world, an unrivalled source of information, a corner-stone, albeit a small one, of the huge institutional and intellectual edifices which constitute the Christian Church of today. But the doubter is entitled to ask – 'Is it true?' I cannot prove it, I can only testify to it. For nearly thirty years now I have been a patient and painstaking student of the St Mark's Gospel. Week after week, year after year I have been sitting down in front of this gospel seeking to penetrate it, to keep my mind open to it and to be aware of the important critical issues which it raises. I can only say that this exercise has only served to reinforce a conviction that in this gospel we are in the presence of historical, elemental truth. Of course it cannot lay claim to be a total biography of Christ and was never intended to be such, as the fragment from Papias makes clear. Of course there will be inner contradictions which are incapable of being harmonized at this distance from the events recorded. And of course he cannot but have been influenced by the Church of which he was a member, by the liturgy in which he took part, by his journeys with his fellow missionary,

St Paul, and by the theological convictions which had taken root in his mind. He is not, and never could be, an unbiassed observer. There are no unbiassed observers in any field of human knowledge. But of the reliability of his portrait of Christ and of the impression he created upon his fellow Jews, upon the leaders of Israel and upon his own followers, I have no doubt. We are in the presence of an event which has stamped itself indelibly on the mind of St Mark and on the life of the Church of St Mark's day. No man is entitled to indulge his doubts on this matter unless he is prepared to commit himself to laborious but infinitely rewarding days of study.

There is another form of doubt which is not necessarily critical of orthodoxy, nor indeed has any reason to doubt the substantial reliability of the New Testament documents. Rather, it simply does not apprehend the relevance of the discussion. As George Macleod is once reported to have said – 'You have proved it up to the hilt and it doesn't mean a thing.' I confess that I have sometimes preached sermons of which the same could be said; perhaps I am now writing a book of which the same will be said; perhaps I might one day attempt a detailed commentary on St Mark of which the same, with more justice, will be said. This is doubt expressed as a sense of irrelevance – the great institutions of the Church are there but they mean nothing to me. The New Testament is available but I see no reason why I should read it. I am not interested in the matters on which the Church presumes to comment. The great issues which purport to be great do not seem to be great to me. This disdainful attitude is exemplified in St Paul's encounter with Felix, Procurator of Judea.

> After some days Felix came with his wife Drusilla, who was a Jewess; and he sent for Paul and heard him speak upon faith in Jesus Christ. And as he argued about justice and self-control and future judgment, Felix was alarmed and said, 'Go away for the present; when I have an opportunity I will summon you.' At the same time he hoped that money would be given him by Paul. So he sent for him often and conversed with him. But when two years had elapsed, Felix was succeeded by Porcius Festus; and desiring to do the Jews a favour, Felix left Paul in prison. (Acts 24:24–7)

Felix is the archetype of the worldly man, promoted, so we
believe, by stealth to his appointment as Procurator and
concerned, like Pilate before him, at all costs to safeguard his
position in the Roman hierarchy. He has, so St Luke says,
accurate knowledge of the way, but he is confronted by one
who really believes in it, who takes justice and self-control
and future judgement seriously. The man of the world is
always alarmed by the vehemence and enthusiasm of the man
of the Spirit. He is a double-minded man, as St James would
put it, not unaware of the truths which are being proclaimed
but unwilling at any point to come to grips with them in case
his livelihood, prestige, his accepted view of himself should
be challenged by them. But no man can forever remain indifferent to the portentous challenge of the Gospel to take seriously the realities by which he is surrounded, the uncomfortable intimations of reality alongside the realities of the world,
the sudden stab of pain which alerts him to his own mortality,
the tragic bereavement which arrests his headlong progress
and causes him to think of judgement and the life to come.
Such doubt is not doubt in the Biblical sense; it is worldliness
masquerading as a laudable rationality. It is the final refuge
of the man who will not face up to realities.

I come now to a fourth aspect of doubt, far removed from
the worldliness which I have just been describing. It is a
doubt which is implicit in all faiths and indeed springs from
it. It is the doubt of a man who does indeed take justice,
judgement and future life seriously but whose faith quails
before the stupendous truths which fight for dominance in his
life. So Bishop Mark Green was able to describe his experience of ministry under the title *A Diary of Doubt and Faith*.
The Russian philosopher, Dr S. L. Frank (in *God with Us*,
Cape, 1946), approaches this particular problem in the
following words:

This is how I see it: the uncertain remains uncertain; to
believe in something uncertain and to affirm as true something which is doubtful is either frivolous – unfortunately,
our life is full of frivolous beliefs for which we have to pay
cruelly – or does violence to our intellect: we 'persuade'
ourselves of something which in reality we go on doubting.
To demand faith in that sense is, strictly speaking, to insist
upon and regard as valuable a certain kind of obstinacy, a

sort of deliberate auto-suggestion inevitably leading to a splitting of consciousness. But surely the first duty of spiritual self-education is to be completely truthful and to draw a clear line of demarcation between 'yes' and 'no', between the certain and the doubtful. I can see nothing either valuable or necessary in an obstinate defence of unverified convictions and a readiness to admit the uncertain as true. Such an attitude of mind is inevitably connected with inward doubt; if one is honest with oneself, the 'I believe' frequently turns out to mean 'I don't believe but I should like to believe and I persuade myself that I do' – and this is certainly a sin before God as the Spirit of Truth. As Byron once said in his youth, 'the first attribute of the Deity is truth.'

This is in line with the attitude, explicit or assumed, in the Old Testament. One of the secrets of the endurance of Israel is that its adherents have never been asked to assent to any series of propositions or to any system of theology. What concerns them is not orthodoxy but orthopraxis. Unfaithfulness is not expressed in terms of doubt but in terms of disobedience to a received truth. And that truth is, as Dr Franks says later in the same chapter – 'In the last resort faith is the encounter of the human heart with God, God's manifestation to it.' The life of Israel was built upon an encounter with the living God at the Red Sea and Sinai, and the lives of its greatest representatives were built upon individual encounters with the living God. They were not required to believe but to act and obey. But to do so exposes such a person to a giant mystery which he can never hope to penetrate, much less to assimilate. His problem is not how to believe but how to survive the belief which he already has. Job was a loyal believer who refused to curse God in his adversities; his doubts were not of the rational kind, questioning the existence of God, but of an instinctive kind, challenging his whole understanding of life. In Job's case, as in so many others, that kind of doubt does not yield except to a transcendent experience of God Himself, as it is recorded in Job 38–42. There is indeed a kind of doubt which actually verifies the faith from which it springs. 'Bishop Blougram's Apology' by Robert Browning, gets as near to the understanding of this problem as any other work I know. Here is Bishop

Blougram (modelled, so we are told, on the life of Cardinal
Wiseman) speaking to his sceptical friend at the dinner table.

> And now what are we? unbelievers both,
> Calm and complete, determinately fixed
> To-day, to-morrow, and for ever, pray?
> You'll guarantee me that? Not so, I think.
> In no-wise! all we've gained is, that belief,
> As unbelief before, shakes us by fits,
> Confounds us like its predecessor. Where's
> The gain? how can we guard our unbelief.
> Make it bear fruit to us? – the problem here.
> Just when we are safest, there's a sunset-touch.
> A fancy from a flower-bell, some one's death,
> A chorus-ending from Euripides, –
> And that's enough for fifty hopes and fears
> As old and new at once as Nature's self,
> To rap and knock and enter in our soul,
> Take hands and dance there, a fantastic ring,
> Round the ancient idol, on his base again, –
> The grand Perhaps!

Miguel de Unamuno puts it more succinctly – 'Life is doubt,
and faith without doubt is nothing but death.'

The kind of doubt I have been describing is really no more
and no less than the collapse of the human mind before the
mysteries of existence. It is endemic in us all, believer and
unbeliever alike. But the believer does have the inestimable
advantage of perceiving within the dark mysteries of life
glimpses of radiance which tell him all manner of things shall
be well. In the very depths of despair he can still invoke a
God who has been revealed to him in the life of Jesus of
Nazareth. At the end of his tether he knows that he cannot
drift outside God's love and care.

George MacDonald, a strange genius of a man, a contemporary of Robert Browning and the inspirer of C. S. Lewis,
Charles Williams, and many another modern writer, kept a
diary. It is called *The Diary of an Old Soul*, but originally it
had the sub-title 'A Book of Strife'.* The diary is the diary
of a deeply committed believer who had fought his way

*Published by Arthur C. Fifield, 1905.

through many thickets of unbelief, plumbed the depths of many a personal disaster, suffered the pangs of faith – and doubt. Here is his entry for September 12th:

> Can anything go wrong with me? I ask –
> And the same moment, at a sudden pain,
> Stand trembling. Up from the great river's brim
> Comes a cold breath; the farther bank is dim;
> The heaven is black with clouds and coming rain;
> High soaring faith is grown a heavy task,
> And all is wrong with weary heart and brain.

George MacDonald exemplifies in his own person many of the issues which we have been discussing in this chapter. He had his doubts about many of the theological structures erected rather precariously in the Bible – 'legal cobwebs spun by spiritual spiders' as he calls them. It was because he dared to criticize the orthodoxy of his day that he was deprived of his first pastorate. Like many another minister he felt the cold draught of continental critical theology of the Bible, but his *Unspoken Sermons* are testimony to the extent to which he transcended these problems in his devotion to the living Christ, adequately though not wholly revealed, as he held, in the New Testament. But indifference to the great issues raised by the Bible would have been unthinkable for him. He had suffered deprivation and poverty, sickness, pain and bereavement. He had seen glittering reputations brought to nothing and good men persecuted. His waking moments were filled with the still, sad music of humanity. His was never the doubt which gave rise to indifference. But he had doubts nevertheless, and it is significant that his own title for the diary was 'A Book of Strife'. It reveals not only the mind but the heart of a man struggling with the immensities, resisting the evidence of sense, and rising to a contemplation of the eternal beyond the veil, bearing in his own body the pangs of incurable illness, holding fast to faith, silent at the end for nearly seven years but at peace, waiting for the coming of his Saviour. It is thus that this man of faith writes of his doubts:

> . . . a man may be haunted with doubts, and only grow thereby in faith. Doubts are the messengers of the Living One to rouse the honest. They are the first knock at our

door of things that are not yet, but have to be, understood; and theirs in general is the inhospitable reception of angels that do not come in their own likeness. Doubts must precede every deeper assurance; for uncertainties are what we first see when we look into a region hitherto unknown, unexplored, unannexed.

(*Unspoken Sermons*, 2nd Series,
Longmans Green, 1886)

This is indeed Christian confronting the giant Despair in Doubting Castle.

MAN-MADE SHRINES

The Word which 'speaks with authority' is what Leibniz called 'the one divine Reality substantial to the manifold world of things and lives and minds'; it is the Eternal Gospel. It is a Word apprehended, unlike the probability findings of brain, by ratiocination, but by the divination of the person made whole, conveying, not abstract knowledge for reason, but concrete wisdom of and for life. It is itself life and conveys life as, originally, the 'Hail' was conceived as conveying health and the 'Sala'am' of the Syriac world peace from person to person.

To that aboriginal Word historic Churches and traditions are secondary and subaltern. They are man-made shrines where that Word is or should be revealed and adored. They do not create or possess that Word; they are created and possessed by it. When the shrine rather than the Word is adored, historic and human Churches rather than this eternal Christ-Word, that is idolatry.

Melville Chaning Pearce (*Deep Church*, Gollancz, 1952)

7   FAITH AND THE CHURCH

Of all the doubts exposed on the radio by 'Priestland's Progress' and by the correspondence that followed it, the most persistent was concerned with the Church itself. In his book Gerald Priestland conveys this sense of doubt in the chapter 'The Church you love to hate'.

> While church-goers spend much of their time describing God, praising God and petitioning Him, non-churchgoers have plenty to say about why the churchgoers are phonies: they burn people at the stake for heresy, *fail* to burn people at the stake for heresy, represent the Tory party at prayer, represent the Communist party in the pulpit, lavish vast sums on vestments and palaces, tell fairy stories that none of them believes, call each other names, frighten little children with threats of hell-fire, cause civil war in Ireland and pretend to be better than others when in fact they are just as bad. (*Priestland's Progress*, BBC, 1982)

So, we happen upon the curious paradox that the organization which exists, so the New Testament tells us, to preach the Gospel to every creature, is itself one of the most serious obstacles to faith in that Gospel. This must call for some heart-searching by those in responsible positions in the Church, but it calls for some explanation too if we are not to beat our breasts in vain.

No one should under-estimate the degree of hostility that exists towards the Church. Gerald Priestland's correspondents included a few who resisted any kind of religion out of conviction, regarding it as an enemy of progress, some who had had an unfortunate experience of the Church at a critical moment in their lives, many who knew little or nothing about the Church and simply repeated well-worn anathemas against it – but more disturbingly, not a few deeply religious people whose aspiration after truth and holiness found, so it would seem, no echoes in the Church of God. On the whole, the most damaging criticism of the Church emerges from those who long for the truth which the Church is supposed to proclaim and do not find it there. This is a quotation from 'A Journal from 1st May to 30th September 1941' written by a man consumed with a flaming desire for the truth, who nevertheless recoils from the Church in which he might have been expected to find it. This is part of the entry for the 3rd July 1941. The Church, he says, represents:

> a Christianity not 'separate' from the world, but come to terms with it, not 'led by the Spirit', but guided mainly by morality and 'good form'. It is Christianity tamed and domesticated; for the rage and splendour of Spirit-possessed men we find 'decency', mild manners, kindliness, for the flame of Christ's love, amiability, for the passion of Paul's 'charity', 'charities'. And the Spirit has left it; power is gone from it – that 'dunamis' which can alone 'overcome the world'. And, as such, it grows sodden, soft, corrupt, emasculate and emasculating. (Nicodemus, *Midnight Hour*, Faber, 1942)

My wife and I, quite independently of each other, happened upon this book and read it – and have never recovered from it. In the springtime of my own faith that is exactly how I felt about the Church. When, therefore, as sometimes happens, young clergymen have come to see me and have confessed that they were disillusioned with the Church, they were surprised to find that I was not surprised. They were not proposing, as they might have been a century ago, to become Roman Catholics. That traffic has long since ceased. They were not even ten years ago, proposing to join the Pentecostalist Church. To them the Church in all its manifestations had become a problem for faith. But as I sat there in my study confronted with these still enthusiastic, but angry, young men I was asking myself, and I occasionally asked them – where did you get your illusions? Had they never read of Moses and the Church in the wilderness? Were they unaware of the running battle between the religious establishment and the prophets in the life of Israel? Did they never read in the New Testament of the unceasing hostility of official Judaism to our Lord Himself, a representative of all true religion? Yes indeed, this had been part of their theological education but that was before the gritty experience of daily encounter with the Church at St Andrew's or St Agatha's or St Ambrose.

So it is often the clergy who feel most painfully the contrast between the Church of their dreams and the Church of their waking hours. That experience is reflected in a remarkable book by J. W. Stevenson, a Presbyterian minister, called *God in My Unbelief* (Collins, 1960). Here he is describing his institution in the ancient parish of Crainie:

> I saw them first through the tinted glass of the vestry window . . . I had made my vow in another country church three months after my father's death. In that moment the years of uncertainty had seemed to be put behind me as I knelt at the Communion table beside which his body had been laid. But I had found, like others, that it is one thing to wish to serve the highest and another to be willing to be made fit for the serving.
>
> Even on this day, within Crainie Kirk, with its one ancient wall and the remainder of its structure adapted to create an extra 'laird's loft' a hundred years before, different voices were speaking in the name of the Church at the moment when most of all I wanted to hear one voice clearly.
>
> The words of Scripture were in my ears, giving me my warrant – that I was to stand before these people in Christ's stead, beseeching them to be reconciled to God. The ancient prayer was said for me, that I might present myself a living sacrifice. Assurance was sought from me that zeal for the glory of God, love to the Lord Jesus Christ and a desire for the salvation of men were my 'great motive and chief inducement' in entering the office of the holy ministry.
>
> But another voice was counselling me in other tones. I must not expect miracles; I must hasten slowly; I must keep the peace . . . . The minister of a neighbouring parish was giving me my 'charge' from the plush-backed pulpit set against the austere Norman walls. He was speaking out of long experience of the ways of men in these upland glens, and I know he loved the Kirk. But he seemed to leave me thinking that the great factor in my ministry would be my

capacity to handle difficult situations tactfully and to keep on good terms with all my people.

Few of us in the ministry of the Church will have altogether escaped the tension that is represented in that passage – the tension in the radical demands of the Gospel and the face of the Church as it is seen through the tinted glass of the vestry window. Few of us will escape the sense of unreality which sometimes accompanies a carefully prepared, deeply felt sermon from the pulpit as the words bounce harmlessly from head to head in the pews. Is it possible to live creatively rather than negatively with this tension? Is there any standing room between the Church as it is and the Church as God intended it to be?

Between the time that I read the journal *Midnight Hour* and found myself deeply in sympathy with it, and the time that I sat as a bishop in my study listening to the young man who was disillusioned with the Church, certain changes had taken place in my own mind. It is never easy to judge how far those changes represent proper growth in understanding or a wholly improper accommodation to the ecclesiastical structures for which by then I had some personal responsibility. However, I had been a theological college teacher for several years and I had indeed grappled with the tension between what is and what ought to be in the pages of Holy Scripture itself. I was no longer entirely 'naked to my enemies'.

Indeed one of the persistent issues which arises out of the Old Testament is the relationship between the Church and the prophet, which has its origins far back behind the so-called period of the prophets. The Pentateuch itself is a study of the relationship between a prophet (Moses) and what the writer to the Hebrews calls 'the Church in the wilderness'. The people of Israel had come out from Egypt in response to the prophetic word and had come out by the mighty hand of God with signs and wonders. They had crossed the Red Sea and found themselves now in the wilderness, led on their way by a pillar of cloud by day and a pillar of fire by night. They fed on angels' food, the manna from Heaven. They were protected from their enemies. But it was not long before the 'Church in the wilderness' was lamenting the flesh-pots of Egypt and wishing to return to them. It was not long before they had forgotten the mighty works of God and, with the connivance of Aaron, were worshipping the works of their own hands. It was the prophet Moses who still kept pure in his mind the vision of the Promised Land and persistently and painfully edged his people towards it. But he paid a heavy price, in terms not only of physical and mental hardship but in terms of spiritual impoverishment. Tempted to, and ultimately succumbing to, impatience with the people of God he is denied the privilege of leading his people into the Promised Land.

> And the Lord said to Moses that very day, 'Ascend this mountain of the Abarim, Mount Nebo, which is in the land of Moab, opposite Jericho; and view the land of Canaan, which I give to the people of Israel for a possession; and die on the mountain which you ascend, and be gathered to your people, as Aaron your brother died in Mount Hor and was gathered to his people; because you broke faith with me in the midst of the people of Israel at the waters of Meribathkadesh, in the wilderness of Zin; because you did not revere me as holy in the midst of the people of Israel. For you shall see the land before you; but you shall not go there, into the land which I give to the people of Israel. (Deuteronomy 32:48–52)

This pattern adumbrated in the Pentateuch, and no doubt owing something to the later prophetic tradition, was to be repeated over and over again in Israel's history. Most of the prophets, under varying historical circumstances, nevertheless had this in common – they were called to battle ineffectively with the stubborn hearts and minds and ineffectual wills of the people of God. So far from encouraging people to 'come to Church' one of them, Isaiah, in his own dramatic way speaks in God's name, counselling them to stay away:

> Hear the word of the Lord,
>   you rulers of Sodom!
> Give ear to the teaching of our God,
>   you people of Gomorrah!
> What to me is the multitude of your sacrifices?
>   says the Lord;
> I have had enough of burnt offerings of rams
>   and the fat of fed beasts;

I do not delight in the blood of bulls,
  or of lambs, or of he-goats.

When you come to appear before me,
  who requires of you this trampling of my courts?
Bring no more vain offerings;
  incense is an abomination to me.
New moon and sabbath and the calling of assemblies –
  I cannot endure iniquity and solemn assembly.
Your new moons and your appointed feasts
  my soul hates;
they have become a burden to me,
  I am weary of bearing them.

(Isaiah 1:10–14)

The process reached its horrifying climax in the words of our
Lord Himself to the Church of His day, 'You are the sons of
those who murdered the prophets' – and within a few days
was Himself murdered by the people of God He had come to
save. So the young man in my study had history on his side
if he had been able to perceive it amidst all the academic
complications of the Old Testament.

But you may say, and rightly, that this is a characteristic
of the ancient people of God, without parallel necessarily in
the history of the Church of Christ. We ought not to be so
sure, because there are indications of that same tension
between the prophet and the Church, the Spirit and the
institution, in the New Testament narrative as well. I draw
your attention to one, dare I say, indisputable fact. In
Matthew 28:10 and Mark 16:7 the disciples are commanded
by the Risen Christ to go to Galilee. In John 21 the account
is given of an appearance to the disciples by the Sea of
Tiberius. But in Luke 24:49 those same disciples are
commanded to stay in Jerusalem, a command which is reiter-
ated in Acts 1:3–4 – 'To them he presented himself alive after
his passion by many proofs, appearing to them during forty
days, and speaking of the kingdom of God. And while staying
with them he charged them not to depart from Jerusalem,
but to wait for the promise of the Father.' Now of course it
is possible to 'harmonize' these accounts to suggest that we
are in the presence of consecutive events rather than opposing
events, that they went to Galilee and then came back to

Jerusalem, or that they stayed in Jerusalem and went to Galilee. But in terms of the documents themselves we would have to observe that St Luke, so faithful to his Markan source in so many other respects, here quite explicitly disassociates himself from it. The older tradition of the resurrection appearances was connected with Galilee. St Luke, for reasons of his own, wishes to emphasise that the resurrection appearances took place exclusively in Jerusalem. What are we to make of this contrasting view of the early history of the Christian Church? There is indeed an early tradition critically evaluated in volume 1 of E. P. Sanders' book, *Jewish and Christian Self-definition* (SCM Press, 1980), that the early Christians at the fall of Jerusalem left the city altogether for Galilee and ultimately for Pella. We lack the historical resources to provide any connected history of the movements of the early Christians in the first century. There is no doubt that St Mark, followed by St Matthew and St John, associate the early developments of the Church with Galilee. It was on a mountain in Galilee that Jesus committed his authority to the Church – 'All authority in heaven and on earth have been given to me. Go therefore and make disciples of all nations, baptizing them in the name of the Father and of the Son and of the Holy Spirit, teaching them to observe all that I have commanded you; and lo I am with you always, to the close of the age' (Matthew 28:18–20). Given the lack of historical certitude, to which St Luke would have been as subject as we are, we will have to take seriously the possibility that St Luke was not dealing only in historical categories but in theological categories. For Mark, Galilee was the fountain-head of Christian mission, for St Luke it was Jerusalem.

Galilee and Jerusalem stand for two different images in the mind. They are not just geographical locations. They conjure up different memories and contrasted aspirations. Galilee in the gospels, both Markan and Lukan, is the place of enthusiastic response to Christ's ministry – the sick were healed, demons driven out, the dead were raised, and fervent hopes of the kingdom were awakened. It was there that Jesus 'saw Satan as lightning fall from heaven'. It was the place of vision and hope. Jerusalem was regarded by the people of Galilee much as London is regarded by the people of the North today. It was indeed the site of the great Temple, but it was also a centre of intrigue where learned ecclesiastics walked down corridors of power and manipulated the government of the day. It was a place dominated by the proud structures of men, with religion enclosed within high walls, administered by distant potentates, temperamentally out of sympathy with the high excitements of their Galilean brethren. So the only untoward intervention in the onward march of Christ in Galilee was the solemn deputation to Jerusalem, seeking to discredit this manifest movement of the Spirit. So unfamiliar with the Jerusalem scene were the disciples of Christ that they stood there after the triumphal entry open-mouthed and over-awed before the massive structures of the city. The religion of Galilee was of a charismatic, adventurous, unpredictable, spontaneous kind, unstructured, uncontrolled – it was of the kind which the young clergyman in my study would have wholeheartedly embraced. This is what he expected the Church to be.

We have to ask then what was in the mind of St Luke when he insisted on Jerusalem as the launching pad of the Christian movement. His account of the Ascension insists that the disciples were to be 'witnesses in Jerusalem and in all Judaea and Samaria and to the end of the earth'. It is reasonably certain that St Luke was writing after the fall of Jerusalem in AD 70 – an event which for its effect both upon Judaism and upon Christianity is without parallel. By the time of writing, therefore, all that remained of Jerusalem was a few ramshackle and blackened ruins in which a few Jews and Christians eked out a miserable existence. Gone was the 'glory'. The faith of Judaism was now represented in the rabbinic centre at Jamnia and (it could be true) such Christians as could be found in Palestine at all were to be found in Galilee or Pella.

St Luke was a Gentile, and so, it may be believed, a convert to the Jewish faith before he became a convert to the Christian faith. For him, therefore, Jerusalem was an image in the mind rather than a place on the ground, much as it is today to the pious believer who in the end much prefers his image in the mind to the Jerusalem on the ground. For St Luke, therefore, Jerusalem stood for stately ritual which had been enacted on Mount Zion as far back as the ancient records went. It was the consummation of the movement that began with the call of Abraham and associated Abraham with Zion and the Melchizedek whom he encountered there, the Priest of God

Most High. Jerusalem had a long history, it was the magnet of the nations; it was the city from which the River of God flowed for the healing of the nations. It was, according to the imagination of pious geographers, the centre of the earth. This was important to Luke because as a companion of St Paul he was well aware of the new-fangled transient religions which so dominated the Greek world of his day. After all, one of the attractions of Paul's teaching at Athens was, in the view of the Athenians, that he was talking about some new thing. Could not the Christian movement be just another new thing which would pass away like the rest, leaving only a few relics behind? What was to happen to these tiny vulnerable congregations, so fretful and divided, in Ephesus, Pergamos, Thyatira, Sardis, Philadelphia and Laodicea? Would they survive the sad divisions in their own ranks or the unwanted attentions of the Roman imperial power?

St Luke was not to know of course that the Christian Church would remain long beyond his lifetime a sect of the Jewish religion and would continue to enjoy a privileged status thereby. But it is not difficult to see, under these circumstances, why St Luke wished to earth the Church in the ancient religion of Israel as it was represented by the city of Jerusalem. For him, the long antiquity thereby achieved would give substance to the hope of a long future. St Luke to give him his due, immeasurably enlarged the range of vision which was implicit in the coming of Jesus of Nazareth. But, to give him his due also, he struck a note which jarred upon the nerves of those who embraced the free unstructured spontaneous religion of Galilee. The note has been jarring ever since. But must it be so? Do we have to be disillusioned with the Church?

I commend to the serious student a book to which I have owed a great deal in my own study of this particular issue. It is *Two Biblical Faiths: Protestant and Catholic* by F. J. Leenhardt, Professor of New Testament in the University of Geneva (Lutterworth, 1962). It would be an impertinence to try to summarize it, but I realize that it is likely to be out of print and as a paperback may not have survived into the second-hand bookshops. The following quotation gives you something of the flavour of the book and at least indicates the nature of the contrast which is drawn by the title.

Abraham lived out the faith of the nomad which he was; his God cannot be confounded with anything of what exists, nor with anything of what He grants. He is, only in the act of His speaking. His word actualizes His promise and realizes His presence. He is not present in what He has said, but in what He says. He is not a God who has ceased to speak, but a God who speaks. When faith translates this dynamic, actual, and present word in terms borrowed from human speech it can give but a clumsy, distorted, inadequate idea of it, in the last analysis a mere dead letter. The word of God is received in faith as a manifestation of power, an act. When God speaks He acts, and His action always transcends what man can convey in language, what God has said. The faith of an Abraham refuses to find support in the traces left by the living word of God in human speech; it disowns the constructions which reason might build on the words which reflect its inner certitude.

Hence faith of the Abrahamic type tends to remove any confusion of the word of the promise with anything human, earthly, factual, historical. It aims at pure interiority. The action of God cannot be stabilized, localized, represented, since it remains ever transcendent. God is nowhere, except in the act itself of His revelatory intervention, that is, in what He says when He summons a soul. There is only one temple worthy of Him, that is the sphere where His word is heard and received; in other words, the heart of the believer. One does not encounter God by entering into some sacred area; one encounters Him by listening to Him: faith is born of hearing (Rom. 10:17). The sole place in which God dwells is the hearts of His people; His only house is where His children are, a spiritual edifice built of living stones (1 Pet. 2:5).

The fundamental unity which binds the faith of Abraham to that of Moses does not, as we have already seen, involve a uniformity in the two types of revelation of which these two great figures are the bearers.

The conditions in which Moses apprehended the revelation of which he was the object clearly indicate its basic character. This revelation brings into play a bush, a mountain, and a storm. One must pierce the symbol to divine its underlying meaning and be able to read the intention which lies beyond the external setting. We must, however, in the first place emphasize the character of externality which marks this revelation. Unlike the word addressed to Abraham which reached the patriarch directly in the secret depths of his conscience, without the use of any intermediary whatsoever, here is a word which has recourse to mediation through external things. Moses' attention is awakened and he becomes involved through facts which are expressed in the sphere of concrete realities. The word of Abraham's God is purely interior; this God is present because He speaks, He is present in His word, and His word is supported by nothing and leaves no trace. The God of Moses is revealed by means of instruments which are raised to the dignity of efficacious signs, and these instruments subsist independently of that act of speaking which they signify, which they both herald and recall ... The faith of Moses has special insight into the fact of continuity, the fact that God enters into the horizontal process of history, and that His pity manifests His fidelity by embodying that fidelity in the very contingent and relative realities of this world.

Professor Leenhardt would be the first to concede that the contrast he makes cannot be accurately located within the Old Testament, given the complex documentary history of the Old Testament. There is no doubt in my mind that he offers us a scenario with which many clergy and indeed many of Gerald Priestland's correspondents would recognize and identify with. Yes, that is what they mean – the Church they experience down the road or the Church they read about from afar is seriously at variance with the kind of 'community of the Spirit' which in their hearts they look for. The title of the book, however, could be misleading. For example, a dividing line does not correspond to any dividing line between the Churches, viz. Catholic/Protestant, but is within the Churches. Cardinal Suenens is one amongst many, although one of the most distinguished, who represents the Galilee spirituality over against the powerful Jerusalem-style ecclesiastical structures which are otherwise so characteristic of the Roman Church. And the issue goes back far behind any nomenclature which is associated with the Reformation. Charles Williams, in his book *The Descent of the Dove* (Religious Book Club, 1939), an original and highly illuminating view of Church history, makes this point: 'The defeat of Montanism exhibits the Church as an Institution more clearly than any other moment, and an Institution committed to reconciliation (not compromise) with ordinary men.'

This movement takes us back to the latter half of the second century. It was a movement of the Spirit orchestrated by a man named Montanus in Phrygia, which laid great emphasis upon prophesy and tongues and has been regarded as an attempt to recover the primitive fervour of the Church in the face of growing institutionalism and secularization. Even Tertullian, that formidable advocate of the Latin Church, became a member of the Montanist party and it survived under various forms for several centuries. There is a sense in which it was never defeated and lives on to challenge the great institutions, whether they be Protestant or Catholic.

What comfort, if any, are we to gain from this dual spirituality which Leenhardt discerns in the Old Testament and is certainly there to be discerned in the New Testament as well? Must we say that the structures of the Church have quenched the Spirit and only quake again occasionally when the Spirit erupts in some great event or in some great person? If that is so, there is very little hope that the Church will ever recover the multitudes represented in 'Priestland's Progress'. The best we can hope for is that here and there a community of Christians, fired with the Spirit, may provide a home for this or that lost soul looking for the kind of experience for which the author of *Midnight Hour* looked in vain. Or are we perhaps at a stage in Christian history when the long Mosaic hegemony is threatened by the return of Abraham who heralds a new era of the Spirit? That indeed would be a creative view of the matter insofar as the influence of the great institutional Churches could be regarded as the prelude not to the creating of new institutions but freeing those same institutions from the institutional forms by which they are at present known to the world. Or can we say that Moses and Abraham, Galilee and Jerusalem, need each other? This is a point indeed made by Leenhardt himself in his concluding chapter:

> . . . the spirituality stemming from Abraham develops its promises if the Mosaic spirituality provides it with a sphere in which to act, a material to animate and quicken. On its side, the spirituality stemming from Moses develops its

promises if the Abrahamic spirituality acts upon it as salt and leaven. The word is event; it must emit its resonance, otherwise nothing happens. Yet this word must not get lost in the limitless horizons it unfolds; there must be grouped around him who utters it those who are to hear it; it must in some way be conveyed to their understanding; it must be explained and applied to them. The event demands the genesis of the institution and the event alone justifies the institution, just as the institution presupposes the event and the institution alone can give the event earthly concrete expression. The word without the church is a celestial abstraction; the church without the word is a society of this world.

The same point is made, although in a negative way, by Baron Von Hügel, the famous, though much neglected, Roman Catholic lay theologian who addressed an Anglican audience on the subject 'The place and function within religion of the body of history and of institutions'. He says, after a powerful tribute to George Fox:

It is, surely, a most striking fact that the Society of Friends – with its indifference or hostility to all formal Creeds and Confessions, and with its constant insistence upon the universal light of Christ and love of God towards men, and upon man's supreme duty of a similar love towards God and Man – has not spread, does not spread, indeed does not even simply keep pace with the growth of the population. (*Essays and Addresses*, 2nd Series, Dent, 1921)

It has been a long voyage for the reader and I touch land again at the point at which we embarked – namely, the problem which the Church presents to the man who would live by faith. My experience of the Church began when I was propelled, much against my will, into a Church choir. Anyone who has been a choirboy will know what a powerful immunization that experience can convey – the long services, the meaningless words, and the portentous sermons. Yet for all that, I conceived a great admiration and affection for those who were the officers of this strange, unfamiliar organization – the vicar, so Olympian and at the same time so kind to people in need, so that my own family who had at that time

no formal connection with the Church warmed towards him;
the curate who was friend enough to put up with my seeming
contempt of the Church and to engage with me in a serious
concern for the truth; the RAF chaplain who somehow tri-
umphed over the ambiguities of his position and spoke to the
real needs of those young men at Cranwell; the Bishop, as
he then was, of St Andrews who responded to the clumsy
introduction I had made with loving and perceptive restraint;
the Indian Ecclesiastical Establishment clergyman, whose
home provided me over several years with a cool oasis amidst
the heats of service life. These were the men, functionaries of
the Church which I affected to despise, who watched over
the tender plant of faith which had sprung up in my life. The
curious thing is that many of those who are most critical of
the Church nevertheless have cause to be grateful for and
acknowledge their gratitude to individual men and women
inextricably bound up with the Church – but for the Church
itself they retain an implacable hostility. Perhaps it is true
that the Church is the crib, uncomfortable, unattractive, in
which nevertheless the Christ is laid. I end with a section of
Dorothy Sayers' Festival play called *The Just Vengeance*
(Gollancz), written in 1946, which is perhaps surprisingly
quoted at the beginning of the report by the Doctrine
Commission of the Church of England entitled *Believing in the
Church* (SPCK, 1981). It is about an airman, who has just
died in battle, arriving at the city which for him was his
native Lichfield and finding himself welcomed by townspeople
from the past centuries and required to state his claim to
citizenship:

RECORDER: What matters here is not so much what you did
    As why you did it . . . Can you recite your creed?
AIRMAN; I believe in God . . .
CHORUS: (*picking him up and carrying him along with it*):
    . . . the Father Almighty, Maker of heaven and earth.
    And in Jesus Christ . . .
AIRMAN: No! No! No! What made me start off like that?
    I reacted automatically to the word 'creed' –
    My personal creed is something totally different.
RECORDER: What is speaking in you is the voice of the city,
    The Church and household of Christ, your people and
        country

From whom you derive. Did you think you were
　unbegotten?
Unfranchised? With no community and no past?
Out of the darkness of your unconscious memory
The stones of the city are crying out. Go on.

I suppose I thought myself unbegotten, unfranchised, with
no community and no past, but I found myself responding
to the voice of the city, the Church and household of Christ.

THE SECOND DEATH

Passengers on a ship who are eating, sunning themselves, playing shuffleboard, and engaging in all the usual shipboard activities appear perfectly normal as long as their ship is sailing safely in quiet seas, but these same passengers doing these same things appear deranged if in full view of them all their ship is caught in a vortex that may shortly drag it and them to destruction. Then their placidity has the appearance of an unnatural loss of normal responses – of a pathetic and sickening acquiescence in their own slaughter. T. S. Eliot's well-known lines 'This is the way the world ends/Not with a bang but a whimper' may not be literally correct – there will decidedly be a very big bang – but in a deeper sense it is certainly right; if we do end the world, the sequence is likely to be not a burst of strong-willed activity leading to a final explosion but enervation, dulled senses, enfeebled will, stupor, and paralysis. Then death.

Jonathan Schell (*The Fate of the Earth*, Picador, 1982)

8 FAITH AND THE END

On 29 March 1982, after many delays, the 'Final Report' of the Anglican/Roman Catholic International Commission (ARCIC) was published. Under normal circumstances this report, like the previous reports of the Commission, would have passed almost unnoticed, except in the ecclesiastical corridors of power or in a few lonely journals concerned with ecumenism. It might have won a three-inch column in the pages of *The Times* and a brief reference on the radio news. But a small red-covered official report of 122 pages would not normally have captured the imagination of the news editor of ITN. However, the Pope was about to visit this island and huge, well publicized preparations were in hand. So the Press Conference at Lambeth Palace, which heralded the publication of the 'Final Report', was provided with an excited commentary and accompanied by pictures of the Pope riding in triumph through the street and waving to the multitudes in St Peter's Square. If the commentator was to be believed, reunion between Rome and Canterbury was round the corner. I viewed the programme with deepening dismay at the thought of the letters I would be receiving two days later – from aggrieved Anglicans for whom this news was the first intimation of this remarkable prospect, from furious Protestants rehearsing variations on the 'no Popery' theme. I was even asked to write a Pastoral Letter to the clergy of the Diocese on the subject.

The reality of course was quite different, as the authors of the report themselves well knew. The creation of the Commission (an equal number of Anglican theologians and Roman theologians from all over the world) followed on the now famous visit of the Archbishop of Canterbury to Pope Paul VI in March 1966. The first meeting took place in January 1970, the last in August 1981. The reports the Commission issued in the course of their work demonstrated, if nothing more, a remarkable degree of understanding between the theologians concerned, on a very restricted range of subjects – and that is the important issue for the subject of this particular chapter. They were not exploring the mountain peaks of theology; they did not address themselves, for example, to the great doctrines of creation, incarnation, redemption, atonement, the life of the Spirit and the coming of the Kingdom. They were confined by their brief to the foothills of theology, and their twelve years together was spent in examining the subsidiary, though important, matters of 'Eucharist, Ministry and Authority'. The members of the Commission would be the first to acknowledge that even within this limited field they were able to express the understanding they developed amongst themselves only in elusive and sometimes ambiguous terms which would leave the untrained reader ignorant not only of the results of their discussion but of the reasons for their discussion in the first place. We must ask, therefore, the question – why should these relatively unimportant matters loom so large in the life of the Church and win the costly attention of eighteen men already busy enough in the institutions they happened to serve? And why should the conclusions be so inconclusive?

The answer to this question lies a long way back. Behind the ecclesiastical disputes, which have so often disfigured the Church and led it into schism, lies a basic conflict of opinion about ministry and authority. The Papal claims, so divisive in the life of the Church, are simply a symptom of that problem. But, the reader may ask, cannot we determine this issue by a simple appeal to the New Testament? Faced by this question, many a theologian and many a Biblical scholar will simply turn his face to the wall in despair. None but the most bigoted Roman Catholic apologist would now claim that the Papacy can trace its pedigree back to the New Testament, or to the earliest centuries of the Christian era. At the other end of the scale, even Dr Lindsay's magisterial work *The Church and the Ministry in the Early Centuries* (Hodder and Stoughton, 1902) does not establish beyond dispute that the apostolic ministry was, and always has been, presbyterian in form. So whilst we cannot dissent from the words of a collect used in the ordering of deacons in the Church of England, that Almighty God has by His Divine Providence appointed divers orders of ministers in His Church, we have no means of knowing beyond all doubt what those orders were. But, you may say, is it not strange that the founder of our religion did not make His mind clear about the future ordering of His Church, thus saving us from divisions which He so clearly feared amongst His disciples? Or, if you are more familiar with New Testament scholarship today, you might ask instead – why is it that the New Testament documents arising out of the apostolic era do not at least reflect an order of ministry which was practised by the early apostles, even if not required by our Lord Himself?

These are important New Testament and ecclesiological questions and I must attend to them seriously. The answer to the first question is that our Lord in His divine wisdom did not prescribe a fixed order of ministry which was to be normative for every Christian community or for every age. We may regret it, but we have to live with it. The answer to the second question is that in the absence of dominical instructions, the ordering of ministry seems to have varied from place to place. This is hardly surprising because the early apostles were operating under widely varying conditions. If, for example, a Jewish synagogue in the Diaspora had heard the preaching of St Paul and had been convinced by it, that synagogue would have become, to use a modern term, a 'Messianic community', i.e. a body of people who remained Jewish in practice and organization, but recognized Christ's claim to be the Messiah. In that case the age-old organization of the synagogue would simply have continued, and government would be vested in the 'elders'. This is a situation reflected in the Epistle of St James and many other places in the New Testament. If, on the other hand, as a result of St Paul's preaching in Athens, a group of people had been plucked out of their surrounding paganism to become a congregation of believers then they would not have had the Jewish model by which to run their affairs and would have looked to some other model of leadership and control. That is just one contrast, but there could be others – the contrast, for example, between congregations created in Asia Minor and those in Greece, congregations composed of artisans and congregations composed of or presided over by a Roman aristocracy. The permutations and combinations are endless, and they only emerge by accident from the pages of the New

Testament when, for one reason or another, they become a matter of dispute. The Anglican and Roman Catholic theologians, therefore, who comprised the International Commission can be forgiven their failure to achieve unanimity and clarity on so intricate a question.

If, however, we were to go behind the two questions so far enunciated, we might ask a further question. Why did not our Lord, as He looked down the centuries, do what we may wish He had done and prescribe models of ministry and authority which would provide a focus for unity rather than disunity in the Church to which He gave birth? At this point we begin to leave the foothills of ecclesiastical mayhem and begin to climb amongst the peaks of Christian theology. The plain answer to the question we have addressed to our Lord would have to be that our Lord did not look down the centuries and perceive the multiple achievements and the manifold failures of the Church which He founded. The evidence of the earliest strata of the New Testament suggests that our Lord Himself and His closest followers believed that within the lifetime of the apostles He would return in glory and establish His kingdom on earth. The most striking affirmation of this belief is to be found in St Mark's account of the transfiguration (Mark 9:1): 'Jesus said to them, "Truly I say to you, there are some standing here who will not taste death before they see the kingdom of God has come with power".' This is a striking utterance, striking not only in its implications for the future but in the fact that that utterance is retained in the Gospel despite the growing tendency in the Church of St Mark's day to consign that prediction to a distant future. This is what believers were beginning to say, according to the second epistle of St Peter:

First of all you must understand this, that scoffers will come in the last days with scoffing, following their own passions and saying, 'Where is the promise of his coming? For ever since the fathers fell asleep, all things have continued as they were from the beginning of creation.' They deliberately ignore this fact, that by the word of God heavens existed long ago, and an earth formed out of water and by means of water, through which the world that then existed was deluged with water and perished. But by the same word the heavens and earth that now exist have been stored up for fire, being kept until the day of judgment and destruction of ungodly men.

But do not ignore this one fact, beloved, that with the Lord one day is as a thousand years, and a thousand years as one day. The Lord is not slow about his promise as some count slowness, but is forbearing toward you, not wishing that any should perish, but that all should reach repentance. But the day of the Lord will come like a thief, and then the heavens will pass away with a loud noise, and the elements will be dissolved with fire, and the earth and the works that are upon it will be burned up.

Since all these things are thus to be dissolved, what sort of persons ought you to be in lives of holiness and godliness, waiting for and hastening the coming of the day of God, because of which the heavens will be kindled and dissolved, and the elements will melt with fire! But according to his promise we wait for new heavens and a new earth in which righteousness dwells. (2 Peter 3:3–13)

Observe also how St Paul grapples with this particular issue. The expectation of the second coming was, in many ways, an embarrassment to him insofar as it produced an extravagant response in the minds of those to whom he preached it; they even refrained from marriage or gave up their work in order to be the more ready for the Lord when He came from heaven with the sound of the trumpet. Although St Paul firmly rebuked these extravagances nevertheless he never compromised in his belief that the Lord would come from heaven and would come soon. This alone is powerful evidence for the prevalence of this hope in the early Church as one of the most distinctive elements in the apostolic presentation of the Gospel and the practice of the Christian religion. The hope is enshrined in the Eucharist itself, which is a foretaste of the coming heavenly feast, and the ancient Aramaic word '*maranatha*', which means 'Lord come' became, even amongst Greek-speaking Christians, a rallying cry of faith. In this atmosphere of heated expectation and fervent hope it is surely not surprising that the Christian Church of the first century did not prescribe an authoritative form of ministry to last for ever or indeed concern itself with theological and ecclesiastical niceties of this kind. Any organization which happened to be at hand would do if it served the Gospel, if it enlarged the

mission of the Church and if it summoned men and women
to repent before the great day came. St Paul's speech on Mars
Hill in Athens says it all:

> So Paul, standing in the middle of the Areopagus, said:
> 'Men of Athens, I perceive that in every way you are very
> religious. For as I passed along, and observed the objects
> of your worship, I found also an altar with this inscription,
> "To an unknown god". What therefore you worship as
> unknown, this I proclaim to you. The God who made the
> world and everything in it, being Lord of heaven and earth,
> does not live in shrines made by man, nor is he served by
> human hands, as though he needed anything, since he
> himself gives to all men life and breath and everything.
> And he made from one every nation of men to live on all
> the face of the earth, having determined allotted periods
> and the boundaries of their habitation, that they should
> seek God, in the hope that they might feel after him and
> find him. Yet he is not far from each one of us, for
> "In him we live and move and have our being";
> as even some of your poets have said,
> "For we are indeed his offspring."
> Being then God's offspring, we ought not to think that the
> Deity is like gold, or silver, or stone, a representation by
> the art and imagination of man. The times of ignorance
> God overlooked, but now he commands all men everywhere
> to repent, because he has fixed a day on which he will
> judge the world in righteousness by a man whom he has
> appointed, and of this he has given assurance to all men
> by raising him from the dead. (Acts 17:22–31)

It is interesting to see that the resurrection in St Paul's mind
is not regarded as a demonstration of a past truth but the
guarantee of a future hope, the return in glory.

We are a long way now from the foothills which the ARCIC
theologians so painstakingly explored. We are up there in the
hills, confronted by that giant peak which dominates the
theological scene. And we call that peak 'the end', or the
consummation of the age. It is possible, although we are not
required to do so, to make a distinction between 'faith' and
'order'. The ordering of the Church, the authority of
particular people within it and the organization of the priest-

hood, are essentially matters of contingency. They have no eternal quality, they are interim provisions for the people of God as they wait for the coming of their Lord in glory. If they had been seen in that light these matters might have been less divisive; we would have been spared Papal claims and counter-claims, futile arguments about the validity of ministries between the Churches; we would have been spared many solemn Councils and many Synod debates. But formally at least, in the Church of England we have recovered that ancient dimension at the very heart of the Eucharist in the Alternative Service Book. 'Christ has died,' we say, 'Christ is risen, Christ will come again'. So it is 'as we look for His coming in glory' that 'we celebrate with this bread and this cup His one perfect sacrifice'.

I well remember a debate in the General Synod about this particular passage and recall my astonishment that the Synod should have insisted upon this formula of faith in the face of the arguments of those who would like to have qualified it in some way in the interests of a blander theology. But the Synod was right; it was, in an unexpected way, recovering the mood of the early Church and asserting once more that faith which was the linchpin of early Christian practice. We are bound to ask, therefore, what it is in our twentieth-century experience which prepared the minds of the majority of Synod members, albeit unconsciously, for the reaffirmation of this primitive faith. Why, to use a technical term, has our theology suddenly turned eschatological, i.e. pre-occupied with the end (eschaton)?

But perhaps we ought to ask a prior question – why was this article of faith abandoned in the first place? It is dominant in the New Testament, it is recited in the Creeds, it is, or should be, part and parcel of any systematic theology, and it has a long history. The messianic hope after all dominated the minds of many of the prophets and underlies so ancient a book as the Book of Samuel. There was a whole body of literature, particularly prominent in the Inter-testamental period, which we call for convenience Apocalyptic, which prefigures the dynamic imagery later to be associated with the Second Coming of Christ. The Book of Revelation in the New Testament stands alone in the literature of the early Church but it by no means stands alone in the Sacred Scriptures as a whole. Its own brand of imagery, forged on the

Island of Patmos, is quarried from ancient Jewish and Persian literature which was itself concerned exclusively with the end.

So, to refer back to the previous chapter, if Galilee represents mission in terms of that charismatic movement early on in the life and ministry of Christ, and Jerusalem represents mission in terms of ancient and enduring and growing institutions, Patmos represents mission as the sovereign activity of God operating secretly amongst the power structures of the ancient world and about to break in upon the world with the message of judgement and redemption. No theology is complete which ignores Galilee or Jerusalem or Patmos. The reluctance of the Church to accept the Book of Revelation within its canon of authoritative writing is perhaps significant of the fact that from the second century onwards the Patmos element became more and more subdued, only to emerge in rabid and fanatical form in some of the medieval sects. It would be true today that the morning service of the Church of England, so well ordered and decorous, sits uneasily besides the chapel next door preaching in season and out of season the Second Coming of Christ today – or tomorrow.

There are probably two reasons for the reticence of the great institutional Churches on this particular article of faith. The first does us no credit. The belief in the Second Coming of Christ challenges our pretensions. What value will be our dogmas on the great day when we stand at the judgement seat? Or how important will seem our institutions when every eye is fixed on Christ? Does the Pope's appearance on the balcony in St Peter's Square mean all that much when seen against the background of Christ's appearance in glory? Are we to suppose that the coming in glory must await the consummation of the long process initiated by the 'Final Report' of the Anglican/Roman Catholic International Commission as we inch our way gingerly towards mutual recognition. The point is perfectly illustrated in Morris West's book *The Clowns of God* (Hodder and Stoughton, 1980). It is the story of a Pope possessed with a vision of the coming of Christ, whose utterances threaten the stately processes and careful deliberations of the Curia in Rome. In the end he is presented with an ultimatum – he must either resign or be certified insane. He resigns, retires to a monastery and subsequently travels the world, not on a kind of Papal visit but on a series of secret discussions with those who share his vision of the end. The scenario at the end of the novel is familiar enough in one way – nuclear war is at hand. It is unfamiliar in another way – because the Christ appears. His name is Mr Atha (reminiscent of the famous Maranatha cry of the early Church), and this is how the novel ends, in a conversation with the ex-Pope.

'The answer, please.' Mr Atha prompted him firmly.

'Who am I?'

'I believe,' said Jean Marie Barette, and prayed for a steady tongue. 'I believe you are the Anointed One, the Son of the Living God! . . . B-but . . .' He stumbled and recovered himself slowly. 'I have no mission, I have no authority. I cannot speak for my friends. You will have to teach them, as you have taught me.'

'No!' said Mr Atha. 'Tomorrow I shall be gone about my Father's other business. You must teach them, Jean!'

'How . . . how can I with this halter on my tongue?'

'You are a rock of a man!' said Mr Atha. 'On you I can build a small standing place for my people!'

Any book which essays this huge theme is bound to fail, but it is significant that it should be essayed at all, at about the same time when the Church of England says as part of its liturgy – 'Christ has died, Christ is risen, Christ will come again'.

The second reason for our strange reticence is less culpable. As one wise theologian said, 'If you stand at the station waiting for the train and you observe that grass is growing between the lines, you may be forgiven for wondering whether the train still runs.' That is the problem for most of us. We can acknowledge the dominance of the eschatological idea in the New Testament, we can live with the question marks which that dominance presents to the proud ecclesiastical structures of our day. We can make our affirmations in the Anglican Eucharist but can we sustain this view of life of our transience and our futility in the midst of structures which seem so strong and feel so satisfying.

In January 1982 my wife and I left Bishopthorpe when the threats of flooding appeared to have receded (mistakenly, as it turned out) and went for a few days holiday to our favourite place in Pembrokeshire. In the event it proved to be for more

than a few days. Not long after our arrival the area was
visited by an unprecedented blizzard which blocked all roads
out of the village, interrupted electricity supplies and telephone communication for a week, and induced in us an
uncomfortable sense of our transience upon the earth, our
vulnerability to a minor climatic disorder, our lack of
competence in the basic matters of survival. Day after day
the sun shone brilliantly out of a blue sky but the earth
crackled with frost and wire fences gleamed with crystals of
ice and all animal life was still. Day after day we viewed our
declining stocks of fuel, foraged for driftwood, hoarded our
little supply of candles and went to bed earlier than usual –
to wake up the following morning to another blue sky and a
silent village and nature, as it were, arrested. We could have
been living the other side of the Parousia, the faithful having
been caught up with Christ in heaven. It was not so. When
our fuel ran out a kindly harbourmaster took us off in his
launch and delivered us to the nearest railway station on the
other side of the bay. It was with some relief that we resumed
the ordered everyday business of our lives. I even enjoyed
being back in London and relished the swift smooth journey
from Kings Cross to York. It was nice to be back in the
familiar scene to inspect the damage at Bishopthorpe after
the flood, to resume my duties in the study and write solemn
letters about solemn ecclesiastical affairs. To live with the
Parousia is to live painfully with the unfamiliar and the unpredictable, measuring all our activities in the light of that event,
willing to surrender the securities of the past for the insecuri-
ties of the future, delivered up to a dangerous freedom. This
is how a distinguished theologian* of our own day puts it:

The more Christianity became an organization for discipleship under the auspices of the Roman state religion and
persistently upheld the claims of that religion, the more
eschatology and its mobilizing, revolutionizing, and critical
effects upon history as it has now to be lived were left to
fanatical sects and revolutionary groups. Owing to the fact
that Christian faith banished from its life the future hope
by which it is upheld, and relegated the future to a beyond,
or to eternity, whereas the biblical testimonies which it

*Jurgen Moltmann in *Theology of Hope*, SCM Press, 1967.

handed on are yet full to the brim with future hope of a messianic kind for the world, – owing to this, hope emigrated as it were from the Church and turned in one distorted form or another against the Church.

In actual fact, however, eschatology means the doctrine of the Christian hope, which embraces both the object hoped for and also the hope inspired by it. From first to last, and not merely in the epilogue, Christianity is eschatology, is hope, forward looking and forward moving, and therefore also revolutionizing and transforming the present. The eschatological is not one element of Christianity, but it is the medium of Christian faith as such, the key in which everything in it is set, the glow that suffuses everything here in the dawn of an expected new day.

But the promise of the Parousia is perhaps not best conceived in the language of theology but in the language of poetry. So for me, the richest evocation of this great hope in my own spiritual life is the poem by Edwin Muir entitled 'The Transfiguration' (*Collected Poems*, Faber, 1964):

> But he will come again, it's said, though not
> Unwanted and unsummoned; for all things,
> Beasts of the field, and woods, and rocks, and seas,
> And all mankind from end to end of the earth
> Will call him with one voice. In our own time,
> Some say, or at a time when time is ripe.
> Then he will come, Christ the uncrucified,
> Christ the discrucified, his death undone,
> His agony unmade, his cross dismantled –
> Glad to be so – and the tormented wood
> Will cure its hurt and grow into a tree
> In a green springing corner of young Eden,
> And Judas damned take his long journey backward
> From darkness into light and be a child
> Beside his mother's knee, and the betrayal
> Be quite undone and never more be done.

Paul Tillich was saying this thirty years ago in his sermon on 'The Shaking of the Foundations'. Earlier than most thinkers he recognized the signs of the times and the direction we would have to take if we were to accord with them. The 'shaking of the foundations' is perhaps a necessary preliminary to the end, which we both dread and hope for.

We happen to live in a time when very few of us, very few nations, very few sections of the earth, will succeed in forgetting the end. For in these days the foundations of the earth do shake. May we not turn our eyes away, may we not close our ears and our mouths and may we rather see through the crumbling of a world the rock of eternity and the salvation which has no end.*

*Paul Tillich, *The Shaking of the Foundations*, Penguin, 1949.

BEING SAVED

. . . a man feels himself to be lost in the very moment when he is on the point of being saved. When God is about to justify a man, he damns him., Whom he would make alive he must first kill. God's favour is so communicated in the form of wrath that it seems farthest when it is at hand. Man must first cry out that there is no health in him. He must be consumed with horror. This is the pain of purgatory. I do not know where it is located, but I do know that it can be experienced in this life. I know a man who has gone through such pains that had they lasted for one tenth of an hour he would have been reduced to ashes. In this disturbance salvation begins. When a man believes himself to be utterly lost, light breaks. Peace comes in the word of Christ through faith.

Martin Luther*

*Quoted in Roland H. Bainton, *Here I Stand* (A Life of Martin Luther), Hodder and Stoughton, 1951.

9   FAITH AND SALVATION

Paul Tillich was right. In these days when the foundations
of the earth do shake, few of us will succeed in forgetting the
end. But the man of faith need not try to forget the end; for
him it is the consummation of a long process, painfully
wrought out through geological time and human history. The
Book of Revelation makes a fitting end to the process of
Creation which is a subject of theological reflection in the
first book of the Bible – God saw everything that He had
made and it was good (Genesis 1:25). The promise inherent
in the beginning is gloriously fulfilled in the end.

Meanwhile, however, we walk by faith in a world where
the foundations of the earth shake and where our own lives
are threatened by perils of body, mind and spirit for which
few of us feel adequate. I write in the wake of the Falklands
conflict with its military triumphs and its individual tragedies
– the family bereaved, the young life blighted by injury, the
mind unhinged, the golden prospects dimmed. And then the
bombs go off in London and the streets are strewn with dead
and dying men and women, with the carcasses of dead horses
– and our television screens are full of grief and bewilderment.
But behind the scenes of such spectacular carnage are the
hidden tragedies of husbands and wives who do not get on,
of children alienated from their parents, of long-forgotten
invalids ekeing out a painful existence in some back room. In
the first years of my own ministry I felt the weight of humanity's griefs and sorrows long before I became acquainted with
them in my own experience. It is a world which cannot wait
for the end. It cries out for salvation here and now.

Some of my readers may shudder at the use of the word
'salvation'. For them this is just Church language, the kind
of thing the parson says in the pulpit, a substitute for the
kind of positive action which, so they believe, alone can ameli-

orate our human condition. But before you put the book down in disgust or pass on to the next chapter, observe what the word salvation actually means. It is not by definition a religious word at all. It means as my dictionary has it 'preservation, rescue from danger, calamity etc.' and is often so used in Holy Scripture. The Hebrew word lying behind both the Greek and the English translations is the word '*yasha*'. The word is variously used in the Old Testament to describe salvation from enemies, from illness, from national disaster, from mental anguish. So this religious-sounding word 'salvation' is not so far removed as we might suppose, from events in the South Atlantic, from the Regents Park bomb explosion, from the hospital bed, from the disordered marriage, from the financial crisis which will at some time or other afflict us all.

There are two striking facts about the use of this word and its derivatives in the Scriptures. The first is that it is very common. The Hebrew word in the Old Testament occurs well over 300 times, and the equivalent word in the New Testament occurs over 200 times. This suggests that the human condition has not changed very much over the centuries. Our forefathers of the tenth century B.C. and of the first century A.D. were for the most part ordinary people grappling with the same painful experiences as we grapple with now; they frequently found themselves in need of salvation. The other striking fact is that in the Old Testament the word for salvation is associated more than 120 times with the name of the God whom the Hebrews worshipped. This suggests that they were as conscious as we are of their need of salvation – that they were more conscious than we commonly are of their need of salvation by the hand of God. If I may put it in this technical way, it was the lexical expression of a theological conviction – and it is this association of ideas that we must now explore.

The God of the Hebrews was not the 'God of the Philosophers'. Discussion about the nature of God and about his attributes is notably absent from the Hebrew Scriptures. They were more concerned with the God who acted both in nature and in history, who intervened in the lives of men, who guided, who taught, who healed, who saved. In every documentary source of the Old Testament, however various in terms of language and style and theological perspective, the same truth holds firm – the God whom the Hebrews worshipped was the God of their salvation. This is amply illustrated in the early history of the race, as it is narrated in the Pentateuch. With the Egyptian forces behind them and the Red Sea in front, the people of Israel were commanded to 'stand still and see the salvation of our God'. In the perils and accidents of the wilderness they looked to Him and were saved. The author of the Book of Judges was confident that surrounded by enemies in the Promised Land, it was God who saved Israel from their hands. The author of the Book of Kings was equally confident that even when Jerusalem was threatened by the seemingly irresistible power of Assyria, the Lord would save it:

> Therefore thus says the Lord concerning the king of Assyria, He shall not come into this city or shoot an arrow there, or come before it with a shield or cast up a siege mound against it. By the way that he came, by the same he shall return, and he shall not come into this city, says the Lord. For I will defend this city to save it, for my own sake and for the sake of my servant David. (2 Kings 19:32–4)

The story of the famous encounter between David and Goliath enshrines a truth which seers and prophets, poets and singers, wise men and kings, pressed upon an unwilling and often recalcitrant nation – 'The Lord saves not with sword and spear; for the battle is the Lord's' (1 Samuel 17:47). But of all the seers and prophets, poets and singers, kings and wise men, it is the prophet Isaiah who most consistently associates the name of the God of Israel with the experience of salvation. Over and over again, the noun 'salvation' and the verb 'save' echo through his writings. It is not for nothing that he is called 'the evangelical prophet'. Listen to him as he rejoices in the God of salvation in the following verses:

> You will say in that day:
> 'I will give thanks to thee, O Lord,
>   for though thou wast angry with me,
> thy anger turned away,
>   and thou didst comfort me.

Behold, God is my salvation;
    I will trust, and will not be afraid;
for the Lord God is my strength and my song,
    and he has become my salvation.'

With joy you will draw water from the wells of salvation.
And you will say in that day:
'Give thanks to the Lord,
    call upon his name;
make known his deeds among the nations,
    proclaim that his name is exalted.
Sing praises to the Lord, for he has done gloriously;
    let this be known in all the earth.
Shout, and sing for joy, O inhabitant of Zion,
    for great in your midst is the Holy One of Israel.'

                    (Isaiah 12:1–6)

It must not be thought, however, that the experience of salvation is confined to great national events or wartime miracles. It is written deeply on the hearts of private men and women, far removed from the smoke of battle, with no place in the counsels of the nation, who nevertheless rejoice in the God whom they know as the 'God of Salvation'. The Psalms more than any other section of Scriptures, reveal the attitudes of ordinary men and women as they go about their business, and plough their fields and drive hard bargains in the market place. These verses from Psalm 62 reveal the heart of a man struggling with some unspecified threat to his well-being:

For God alone my soul waits in silence;
    from him comes my salvation.
He only is my rock and my salvation,
    my fortress; I shall not be greatly moved.
How long will you set upon a man to shatter him,
        all of you,
    like a leaning wall, a tottering fence?
They only plan to thrust him down from his eminence.
    They take pleasure in falsehood.
They bless with their mouths,
    but inwardly they curse.
For God alone my soul waits in silence,
    for my hope is from him.

He only is my rock and my salvation,
   my fortress; I shall not be shaken.
On God rests my deliverance and my honour;
   my mighty rock, my refuge is God.
Trust in him at all times, O people;
   pour out your heart before Him;
God is a refuge for us.

(Psalm 62:1–8)

In the Psalms particularly, however, another note is struck which is to become dominant in the later history of Israel and in the writings of St Paul. The more sensitive souls amongst the seers and prophets, singers and poets, the wise men and kings, see that salvation meant more than satisfaction of some pressing physical need or the deliverance from some physical danger; it meant the salvation from those forces within a man which threaten his well-being and destroy his relationships with others. In the minds of such men, God's salvation comes to be associated with salvation from sin. Listen to this heart-felt cry from an un-named penitent:

Make me to know thy ways, O Lord;
   teach me thy paths.
Lead me in thy truth, and teach me,
   for thou art the God of my salvation;
   for thee I wait all the day long.
Be mindful of thy mercy, O Lord, and of thy steadfast love,
   for they have been from of old.
Remember not the sins of my youth, or my transgressions;
   according to thy steadfast love remember me,
   for thy goodness' sake, O Lord.
Good and upright is the Lord;
   therefore he instructs sinners in the way.
He leads the humble in what is right,
   and teaches the humble his way.
All the paths of the Lord are steadfast love and faithfulness,
   for those who keep his covenant and his testimonies.
For thy name's sake, O Lord,
   pardon my guilt, for it is great.

(Psalm 25:4–11)

This association between salvation and sin is slowly devel-

oping in the spirituality of Israel, which reaches its most
poignant expression in the Book of Job. The man Job was an
upright man so it is said, devoted to God, merciful to his
fellow human beings. He experiences a whole series of disasters, culminating in a disfiguring and seemingly mortal
disease. One would have supposed that such a man could
rightly have called upon God for 'salvation' but that salvation
is not forthcoming. He endures long days of pain and isola-
tion, accompanied only by dubious consolations of his so-
called comforters. The experience on the one hand produces
a violent reaction against the God who had failed to bring
him salvation, and on the other a growing awareness of the
deeper issues of life in which he knows himself also to be in
need of salvation. At this point his so-called righteousness,
his piety, his ostentatious service of others, are of no avail.
Listen to him as he addresses the God of his salvation:

> Only grant two things to me,
>   then I will not hide myself from thy face:
> withdraw thy hand far from me,
>   and let not dread of thee terrify me.
> Then call, and I will answer;
>   or let me speak, and do thou reply to me.
> How many are my iniquities and my sins?
>   Make me know my transgression and my sin.
> Why dost thou hide thy face,
>   and count me as thy enemy?
> Wilt thou frighten a driven leaf
>   and pursue dry chaff?
> For thou writest bitter things against me,
>   and makest me inherit the iniquities of my youth.
> Thou puttest my feet in the stocks,
>   and watchest all my paths;
>   thou settest a bound to the soles of my feet.
> Man wastes away like a rotten thing,
>   like a garment that is motheaten.

(Job 13:20–8)

In another age and on another shore, he could have echoed
the words which, when the foundations of my own life shake,
I find myself repeating:

Not the labours of my hands
Can fulfil thy law's demands;
Could my zeal no respite know,
Could my tears for ever flow,
All for sin could not atone:
Thou must save, and thou alone.

Nothing in my hand I bring,
Simply to thy Cross I cling;
Naked, come to thee for dress;
Helpless, look to thee for grace;
Foul, I to the fountain fly;
Wash me, Saviour, or I die.

(Hymn 'Rock of Ages')

We have followed a tortuous, not to say a circuitous route, through the documents of the Old Testament, to establish three points. The first is that the ineffable and mysterious name Jahwe revealed to Israel is not an object of speculation. He is not to be described with adjectives but with verbs. He acts, he intervenes, he saves in the life of the nation and in the life of individuals. The second is that the idea of salvation displays a certain development in the spiritual history of Israel insofar as we can accurately discern that development within the documents of the Old Testament. It begins with somewhat crude ideas of victory in battle, conquest of enemies and of deliverance from natural disasters. For reasons which can, I think, be adduced but can hardly be demonstrated in a short chapter on the subject, those crude conceptions of salvation yield to a more refined view in which salvation is experienced not just in terms of physical safety, but of spiritual deliverance. Those hardy souls who called for salvation in the midst of battle fourteen centuries before Christ yield pride of place to those more reflective souls a thousand years later, who find the burden of their sins more demoralizing than the sight of the enemy at the gate. The third point is that throughout that development one conviction remains constant in the minds of the true Israel as distinct from the sophists and the politicians and the armament manufacturers. It is that only God can save – from physical or moral and spiritual disaster. He was the God of their salvation, without rival, without ally. Living by faith meant putting your trust in the God who alone can save.

If there is any single verse which provides the nexus between the Old and New Testament and shows how integral they are to each other, it is Matthew 1:21 – 'She will bear a son and you shall call his name Jesus, for He will save His people from their sins.' The significance of the verse may not be obvious to the casual reader until he realizes that the name 'Jesus' is a Graecized form of the Hebrew name 'Joshua' and the name Joshua is derived from the word salvation. But observe too that the second half of the verse illustrates the point made in the preceding paragraph – 'He will save His people from their sins.' Even allowing for the fact that the author of the Gospel according to St Matthew was writing in the wake of the developed theology of St Paul, the words are nevertheless all of a piece with the history of the word 'salvation' in the Old Testament and answer the cry of the Psalmists and the Book of Job.

But this verse is a kind of 'trailer' ahead of the main body of the narrative. The narrative itself exhibits most of the aspects of salvation which we have observed in the Old Testament. Jesus, true to His name, saved the disciples when they were in danger of being drowned in a storm on the sea. 'Save us, Lord,' they said, 'we are perishing' (Matthew 8:25). The woman who touched the hem of his garment in the crowd said to herself before she did so, 'If I only touch His garment I shall be saved' – which is the exact meaning of the Greek (Matthew 9:21). When Peter stepped out boldly on to the water in obedience to the command of Christ, and began to sink, he cried out, 'Lord, save me'. He did not have in mind at that moment his eternal salvation, or forgiveness of sin, or redemption. He simply wanted to get out of the water alive (Matthew 14:30). So those who mocked Jesus on the Cross were right when they said, 'He saved others' (Matthew 27:42). Throughout His ministry He was true to His name 'Salvation'. But there is one particularly telling instance in the Gospel According to St Luke which illustrates the other aspect of salvation, to which I have already referred. Here is the account in full:

He entered Jericho and was passing through. And there was a man named Zacchaeus; he was a chief tax collector, and rich. And he sought to see who Jesus was, but could not, on account of the crowd, because he was small of stature. So he ran on ahead and climbed up into a sycamore tree to see him, for he was to pass that way. And when Jesus came to the place, he looked up and said to him, 'Zacchaeus, make haste and come down; for I must stay at your house today.' So he made haste and came down, and received him joyfully. And when they saw it they all murmured, 'He has gone in to be the guest of a man who is a sinner.' And Zacchaeus stood and said to the Lord, 'Behold, Lord, the half of my goods I give to the poor; and if I have defrauded any one of anything, I restore it four-fold.' And Jesus said to him, 'Today salvation has come to this house, since he also is a son of Abraham. For the Son of man came to seek and to save the lost.' (St Luke 19:1–10)

Zacchaeus was not in any physical need. He had not come to Jesus to secure recovery of sight, or healing of body, or the casting out of demons. He had come, we must presume, because beneath the obvious satisfactions of a wealthy man, he was painfully aware of the cost at which that wealth had been acquired. He was, not only in the eyes of his fellow-countrymen but in his own eyes, compromised by his willing association with the government of the day in pursuit of gain. It was the enemy within, not the enemy at the gate, from which he was seeking salvation. Thus it was that in a delib-erately ambiguous phrase, Jesus is able to say, 'Today sal-vation has come to this house' – ambiguous because St Luke would be well aware that the name 'Jesus' meant salvation; but it was true also that the Lord's visit brought salvation, new life for old, to Zacchaeus and his family.

In the Apostolic Church the word 'salvation' begins to acquire the exclusive meaning which we sometimes associate with it today, i.e. (to quote my dictionary again) 'redemption, deliverance from sin and its effects by the merits of Christ's death'. So the congregation on the day of Pentecost were exhorted to save themselves from this crooked generation and in consequence 'the Lord added to their number day by day those who were being saved' (Acts 2:47). However, in one or two instances, the older meaning continues to peep through the narrative although the English translations tend to obscure it. For example, the beggar at the beautiful gate of the Temple, who was healed by Peter in the name of Christ, 'and immediately his feet and ankles were made strong, and leaping up he stood and walked and entered the Temple with them, walking and leaping and praising God' (Acts 3:7–8). But when he is reporting on this incident to the Sanhedrim Peter says, 'If we are being examined today concerning a good deed done to a cripple, by what means this man has been *saved* (healed), be it known to you all and to all the people of Israel that by the name of Jesus Christ of Nazareth, whom you crucified, whom God raised from the dead, by Him this man is standing before you, well.' (Acts 4:9–10). And curiously enough this word appears in its more primitive sense on the lips of St Paul himself in St Luke's account of the ship-wreck. At the climax of the story, Paul said to the centurion and the soldiers 'Unless these men stay in the ship, you cannot be saved' (Acts 27:31).

You will not be surprised to know, however, that in the Pauline epistles themselves, the word 'to save' and the word 'salvation' are never used except in the more developed sense as applying to – 'deliverance from sin and its effects by the merits of Christ's death'. It is in this sense that the word is normally used in Christian dogmatics, ecclesiastical formularies, and certainly in the ordination service. I never take an ordination service without feeling the weight of this great utterance from the exhortation to the priests:

> . . . we exhort you, in the Name of our Lord Jesus Christ, that you have in remembrance, into how high a Dignity, and to how weighty an Office and Charge ye are called: that is to say, to be Messengers, Watchmen, and Stewards of the Lord; to teach, and to premonish, to feed and provide for the Lord's family; to seek for Christ's sheep that are dispersed abroad, and for his children who are in the midst of this naughty world, that they may be saved through Christ for ever. (*Book of Common Prayer*)

We may experience salvation at many points in our lives. There have been many moments in my own when purely out of consideration for my own safety and health, I have asked the Lord to save me. But in the end, when other helpers fail and comforts flee, when we pass through or even approach the dark valley it is for this that my soul longs – to be saved through Christ for ever. It is obvious at that point that salvation is wholly beyond our own efforts to achieve it; no good works, no pious acts, no prayers however fervent, no doctrinal orthodoxy, no membership of the right church, can avail.

It is through faith and faith alone that we are saved. 'Your faith has saved you,' our Lord was apt to say, 'Go in peace' (Luke 7:50; 8:48; 17:19; et cetera). When Martin Luther, a distinguished member of the Augustinian Order, began to insist on this great truth in his lectures on the Epistle to the Romans, he encountered fierce animosity from the Church and earned the title 'the Wild Boar in the Vineyard'. But it is to this 'Wild Boar' that Protestants and Catholics alike owe this surpassing expression of the Gospel – salvation through faith by Christ for ever. To live by faith in this sense is to live by faith in the God of the Hebrews, exhibited by prophets and seers, singers and poets, wise men and kings, and made visible among us by one who received and earned the name 'Salvation'.

But perhaps I ought not to end on that high note in case it should give the impression that salvation is something to be experienced under exceptional circumstances, from exceptional sins and by exceptional people. We must not allow the original Hebrew understanding of salvation to be obliterated by the religious sense we now habitually give to it. The following story illustrates the point.

Some years ago my wife and I were invited to attend the famous Maramon Convention in South India which attracts every year 100,000 members of the Mar Thoma Church to a dry river bed for the whole of a week to listen to the word of God. As we sat in the aircraft awaiting take-off, there were many questions in our minds. I had been to India myself during the second World War, but then I was encapsulated in a service unit which permitted or encouraged little genuine contact with the environment. Were we going to be able to cope with the unfamiliar temperatures, the unfamiliar food and the unfamiliar routines? More to the point, were the lectures I had prepared going to mean anything to a huge concourse of Indians whose thought processes were so different from ours in the West? Were the illustrations so essential to the lectures going to strike any note of familiarity in their minds? How would the interpreters fare with my more extravagant flights of fancy? So we ourselves were in need of salvation, as we viewed the prospect ahead of us.

But there was to be someone else on board in need of salvation. She staggered up the aircraft steps at the last moment, to be ushered by the chief stewardess into the seat next to mine. Could I look after her, the stewardess said. It seems that a clerical dog-collar still identifies the wearer as someone who might be expected to be sympathetic and helpful. I observed with some alarm that my neighbour had a large bottle of whisky with her which was already half empty. She proved to be a very quiet neighbour, unconscious for most of the flight. When she was feeling better the following morning she confided in me the nature of her distress. She was terrified of flying. Was I terrified of flying? No, I was not, but I knew how she felt because I was acquainted with the irrational fear which grips me when I look over a precipice, even if it is only 30 feet high. The thought of flying terrified her; it darkened her days and haunted her nights for weeks beforehand. But there were occasions when she had no alternative but to fly and could only do so if armed with a large bottle of whisky. I offered a few conventional and ineffective remarks.

Like most people I can only think of the right things to say long after the opportunity of saying them has vanished. What I ought to have said to her was – 'Ask God to help you the next time you have to fly.' But, you may say, perhaps she does not believe in God. My reply is that most of us are in that condition most of the time and we shall only come to believe in God insofar as we know Him as the God of our salvation. But simply to have asked God to help her would have put her in touch with the living God of the Hebrews, the God of Abraham, Isaac and Jacob, the God and Father of our Lord Jesus Christ. She would have discovered the reality of God not through any abstruse argument, but through the simple experience of salvation. Trembling and sweating with fear, she might have discovered a mysterious source of peace. Overcome with dread, she might have found strength to climb the aircraft steps without a large bottle of whisky. A cloud might have been lifted from her life, an agony dispensed with. Like Peter, she would have cried out to God as the waves engulfed her and have touched a steadying hand. The experience of salvation when interpreted in this way is often the beginning, not the consummation, of a life lived by faith in the Living God.

THIS PRAYER BUSINESS

Then Miss Watson she took me in the closet and prayed, but nothing come of it. She told me to pray every day, and whatever I asked for I would get it. But it warn't so. I tried it. Once I got a fish-line, but no hooks. It warn't any good to me without hooks. I tried for the hooks three or four times, but somehow I couldn't make it work. By-and-by, one day I asked Miss Watson to try for me, but she said I was a fool. She never told me why, and I couldn't make it out no way.

Mark Twain (*The Adventures of Huckleberry Finn*, Penguin, 1966)

10   FAITH AND PRAYER

Beneath the level of a man's outward history – his career, his public image, his leisure activities – is another history, known intimately to himself alone. He is like a tree planted by the waterside, occupying a visible space in the world but drawing on hidden springs, growing or dying silently, unobserved. He can be described, analysed, adulated or criticized; his life history may be told in an obituary, all of which may bear little relation to his consciousness of himself. He may have won famous victories in the world but knows himself defeated. He may win a great reputation for wisdom or skill but he knows himself to be a nonentity. He may indeed be a holy man of God, a blessing to others, in whose shade they may find coolness and peace, but his inner life may be a turmoil, a pain, a struggle with contradictions and ambiguities. Many an avatar or guru pays a heavy price for the spiritual inspiration he makes available to others.

It is this inner life which must be the subject of any chapter headed 'Faith and Prayer'. It is this inner life which influences our view of the world and our relationship with others, for good or ill. It may be rich or it may be paltry, it may be dull or it may be adventurous. It may be wholesome and life-giving or it may be malign.

It is like the life of a man living in an old mill; the stream is always sounding in his ears, he may become vividly aware of it only in times of spate or in times of drought, but it is always there; when he is working in the garden or painting the windows, when he is lying in bed or watching the television; when he reads or sings. He may endure drastic changes of fortune, totter from riches to poverty or have his name in all the papers, but beneath it all the slowly changing or unchanging stream of his inner life just flows on. Prayer in this sense is not an activity but a state of mind, not a religious experience but a way of life.

The author, therefore, who wishes to write about faith and prayer can only do so in the first instance on the basis of his own experience of that inner life which he himself knows and no one else. So if I now speak in personal terms I do so because there is no other way of providing a model with which the reader may at times identify himself and from which at other times may sharply deviate.

In September 1982 I appeared on a television programme with Yorkshire Television in a series in which Frank Topping was addressing himself, with the aid of guest speakers, to a whole range of important contemporary issues. It is perhaps not without significance that in a series which included well-rehearsed problems of work and leisure, bereavement and healing, there should be one on prayer. I might have expected quasi-technical questions on systems of prayer, or varieties of religious experience, but it did not prove to be that sort of programme. In a large television studio beneath the glare of lights, surrounded by technicians and all the modern apparatus of programme-making, with only a few minutes at our disposal, I was asked two basic questions – How do I know that God exists and is present? How do I know that prayer works? They were questions not designed to provoke an academic argument but to elucidate the realities of one man's inner life, that viewers might identify with or dissent from him.

Mine was, by any standards, a fortunate childhood, born on a farm in the Forest of Dean in Gloucestershire, surrounded by all the evidences of a singularly beautiful countryside, and insulated from the harsh and glaring unrealities to which many a city child is subjected. My life was bounded by the garden and the farmyard and the paddock. My memory, no doubt influenced by the recollections of others, was of long summer days and warm flagstones and the highly distinctive smell of the Scottish collie who was my inveterate companion. That was the beginning of my inner life, not just my outward existence, in which those first impressions were formed, impressions of a friendly world and comforting companionship. Long before I became a practising Christian and began to articulate my faith in words and concepts, I was the happy victim of circumstances which conspired to create an inner life of faith in the ultimate goodness of the universe and of the One who mysteriously abides within it and presides over it.

Subsequently, as a young man working in an office in London, I can recall moments still which evoked those child-hood memories and revived recollections long since subdued by my own passion for rationality and my spirited resistance to religion. When, therefore, I joined the RAF in 1940 I was not devoid of an inner life, though that inner life had little connection with the traditional formulations of the Christian faith. Such faith as I had was inarticulate, unformed, unconsidered, but it was a faith nevertheless, rising unbidden from the circumstances of my own life and, so I would now believe, from the far-seeing design of a loving Providence.

On the evening of the 14th March 1940 I walked out through the office door for the last time. On the following morning, instead of my customary walk from Blackfriars to Chancery Lane, I took the tube to Uxbridge. I have had many long journeys in my time. This was the longest of all – twenty-three stations, clutching a broken-down suitcase with the few possessions that we were permitted to take with us to the recruitment centre. What would it be like? I wondered. Would I pass this way again? What did the future hold for a young man of 22, facing his first long separation from home?

I took with me, amongst my few possessions, two books. One was a Bible, included for no better reason than it seemed the proper conventional thing to do. The other, a book which is unlikely to be known to most of my readers, by a famous American preacher, H. E. Fosdyck. It was called *The Meaning of Faith.* It had been given to me the night before by the curate of the parish, whose friendship I intensely valued, whilst at the same time dissenting fiercely from most of what the curate stood for. He was wise enough not to seek to press me into his mould, or to convince me with powerful arguments. It was enough that he befriended me and gave me a book. The book was organized on the basis of daily Bible readings and comment for three months. I subsequently acquired three other volumes by Fosdyck, organized in the same way, and they became part of my life over my first year in the Forces.

The externals of Service life are the same everywhere and

in every generation – long hours sitting on the end of your
bed waiting for something to happen. Long hours waiting in
queues for the issue of uniforms, or injections, or pay, or food.
It was a life without privacy, though happily enriched by
many an unexpected friendship. A life without privacy, that
is true, but at the same time a life which permitted an intense
personal privacy even in a barrack room with sixty-nine other
aircraftsmen. Strangely enough, the unwelcome routines and
the inexplicable prescriptions of Service life served to heighten
the distinction between what happened on the surface, on the
parade ground, in the lecture room and in the aircraft cockpit,
and what was going on in your own heart and mind. It was
this inner life which provided the continuum beneath the
ever-changing scenery of Service life. It was under those
circumstances that the longings, the aspirations and the
impressions of early manhood began to take shape round the
person who was the subject of all Fosdyck's books.

   Those early years in the RAF, as aircraftman 2nd class,
aircraftman 1st class, corporal in the RAF Police, trainee
pilot, trainee navigator, allowed plenty of time for reflection.
And that reflection gathered itself increasingly around the
person of Christ, aided by a sympathetic chaplain here and
there, enriched by books I happened upon, and shared more
and more by correspondence with the one who was to become
my wife. It is amazing what freedom of mind can be enjoyed
within the seemingly rigid structures of Service life. They
make demands on you, but they support you. They restrict
you, but in that very restriction they encourage an adventurous intellectual life. I lived within the confines of the
barrack room and perimeter fence, but I was free. But free
for what?

   In chapter 3 I described my first encounter with the Christ
of the gospels whilst I was stationed at RAF, Heaton Park,
Manchester over Christmas 1942. From that moment,
without making any positive choice that I can now remember,
I knew that my future life was indissolubly linked with Him.
Such faith as I enjoyed was faith in Him. Such hope as I had
for the future was hope in Him. And now the inner life of
which I had always been dimly aware, acquired a sudden
colour and vigour and sense of direction. Prayer in the
morning, somewhere, somehow, became a necessity. Some
space later in the day became a rich source of solace and

strength. The study of the Bible was tinged with expectancy. Heaven was about us and the Kingdom was round the corner. I recall subsequently six months at Cranwell, subject to laborious hours in front of the morse key, which passed as a dream and was invested with the light and glory of God. It was from Cranwell that I got married, enjoyed a four-day honeymoon and left for Canada with an enthusiasm for the Gospel which no doubt chaplains found very tiresome, and with an eagerness to communicate it which my fellow naviga-tors must have found exceedingly irksome. But for all my naivety it represented an efflorescence of that spiritual life which I had done nothing to deserve and had done little to cultivate.

If this phase of my life had a climax, it was when I found myself later in the war in India, with a precious month's leave to spend. My wife wrote from England suggesting, as a result of reading about the Dohnavur Fellowship, that I might like to spend the month there in Tinnavelly. It was then, and remains now, a lay community devoted to the protection and education of Indian children. The mission compound was like an oasis in the desert, green, well watered, colourful and imbued with an extraordinary atmosphere of prayer and worship. There was no doubt of the source. In a dimly lit room at the heart of the compound Miss Amy Carmichael, the Founder of the Fellowship, was nearing the end of her life on earth, a frail woman now, confined to bed, giving her time wholly to prayer and to the writing of poetry. Around the compound the rich life of an Indian village swirled and eddied, but at the heart was this palpable stillness. I have met only three people in my life who to that extent conveyed a sense of the presence of God – Amy Carmichael of the Dohnavur Fellowship, Brother Roger of the Taizé community, and Pope John Paul II. But for me at that time the life of the Fellowship at Dohnavur was epitomized by the Tower Room, so-called, which from some 50 feet up commanded a view of the western hills. It was a benediction to climb those steps, sit in that room and throw open the window, to feel the cool air of such wind as there was in that stifling plain, and to gaze at the eternal hills.

I speak of the end of that phase of my life. So it seems now, although it scarcely did then. At the time, the war in the Far East stretched out into the immeasurable future, and in my

own view I might have had another seven or eight years living
in the RAF, pursuing my own spiritual quest, free from any
demand for decisions, content to be, without responsibilities
for the world at large. But Hiroshima was no more than
a year away, a year filled with unadventurous duties with
Transport Command in Burma. Long before, when I was
still in England I had signified an interest in the possibility
of ordination to the Church of England, stimulated in part
by that remarkable book *Midnight Hour* by Nicodemus (Faber,
1940). It was a book which my wife and I had each read
without knowing that the other was reading it. It was the
diary of a man with a distinguished career behind him,
captured by the Spirit of God, and able to communicate the
truth as he saw it, in ravishing English prose. In the
enthusiasm of his new discovery he had sought ordination but
had been refused by a somewhat uncomprehending Church. I
met him years after, when I was ordained and he was still a
layman, still seeking, still expounding, still enthusiastic for
the Gospel, a man of deep and rich inner life, to whom many
owe their place in the Christian Church.

But in all the excitements of a war now rapidly nearing its
end, ordination still seemed for me one of a variety of options.
The only option which I had positively excluded was the
option of returning to the office I had left six years before. I
was nervous of ordination and of the professionalism which
seemed to go with it. I was not eager to be associated with
the Church of God which I had long affected to despise. So
when I was invited to attend a selection conference in
Calcutta in 1945 I accepted without enthusiasm and only
determined to go at the very last minute.

It marked the end of one phase and the beginning of
another, for thereafter I was to become in due course an
official of the Church, wearing a special uniform, expected to
say the appropriate thing, committed to an institution of
enormous significance but of sometimes unlovely appearance.
The inner life now had to cope, not with the exigencies of
Service life, the rough and ready companionship of the
barrack room, or with the fleeting friendships that were
contracted under those conditions, but with the heavy
pressures of mind and spirit which bear upon all professional
ministers of the Gospel – the pad-pad of the busy Bishop, or
the intractable relationship problems which the parish priest

encounters day after day in his pastoral charge, or the struggle of the academic theologian to preserve the reality of his own inner life from the threat of a disintegrating theology. I have been in all these situations now and I know of only one resource – the Christ whom I dimly knew as a child, the Christ whom I fervently resisted as a young man, the Christ who spoke to me at Heaton Park, Manchester, through the words of Scripture, the Christ of Dohnavur who summoned me toward the ordained ministry, the Christ of many painful crises since, who is the unfailing companion, not always identified, of my own inner life.

You will say, quite rightly, that I have not written about prayer at all. But then prayer is not to be described in terms of times and seasons, of techniques and systems, words and songs. Prayer is the product of an inner life, which has its source not in our own habits or our own efforts, but in the creative activity of the Almighty God, Himself forming our minds and illuminating our spirits. I am just a tree planted by the water side, lifting up my arms to Heaven, supplied with a rich source which I may tap but cannot create, which I may use but cannot command. Prayer is primarily God's activity in us, rather than our activity in relation to God. Nevertheless, the reader has the right to ask the questions which were the subject of my conversation with Frank Topping on Yorkshire Television in Septembr 1982. The answers I gave then were of little significance and I am not sure that I can improve on them now. But it might be useful to record certain convictions about prayer which proceed not just from personal experience but from a patient study of the Scriptures themselves. On this basis there are certain discriminations which need to be made and I offer them not so much as a guide as a series of markers by which the traveller may judge whether he is on the right road.

The word 'prayer' in the English language has acquired a singularly limited meaning. It suggests something to do with religion, with Churches, form of words with sacred hours before man-made altars. And indeed that is true also of the word which lies behind it in the Greek, a word which is used exclusively of man's intercourse with God, expressed in petitions, pleas, thanksgivings and confession. But when we turn to the vocabulary of the Old Testament the picture is very different. The vocabulary there is rich in its descriptions

of the inner life of patriarchs, prophets and poets. There are
no less than fourteen Hebrew words for which the one English
word 'to pray' has to do service. And they are words which,
with a few exceptions, can be used equally legitimately of
intercourse with men as for intercourse with God. That is a
point of high significance in Hebrew theology. Life is one,
and there is no hard and fast distinction between spiritual
and the natural. In one single chapter, for example in Judges
13, the visitor is described as 'the angel of the Lord', as a
'man of God', as an 'angel of God', as 'the man', and as 'God
Himself'. Here is the passage in full:

And the people of Israel again did what was evil in the
sight of the Lord; and the Lord gave them into the hands
of the Philistines for forty years.

And there was a certain man of Zorah, of the tribe of
the Danites, whose name was Manoah; and his wife was
barren and had no children. And the angel of the Lord
appeared to the woman and said to her, 'Behold, you are
barren and have no children; but you shall conceive and
bear a son. Therefore beware, and drink no wine or strong
drink, and eat nothing unclean, for lo, you shall conceive
and bear a son. No razor shall come upon his head, for the
boy shall be a Nazirite to God from birth; and he shall
begin to deliver Israel from the hand of the Philistines.'
Then the woman came and told her husband, 'A man
of God came to me, and his countenance was like the
countenance of the angel of God, very terrible; I did not
ask him whence he was, and he did not tell me his name;
but he said to me, "Behold, you shall conceive and bear a
son; so then drink no wine or strong drink, and eat nothing
unclean, for the boy shall be a Nazirite to God from birth
to the day of his death".'

Then Manoah entreated the Lord, and said, 'O, Lord,
I pray thee, let the man of God whom thou didst send
come again to us, and teach us what we are to do with the
boy that will be born.' And God listened to the voice of
Manoah, and the angel of God came again to the woman
as she sat in the field; but Manoah her husband was not
with her. And the woman ran in haste and told her
husband, 'Behold, the man who came to me the other day
has appeared to me.' And Manoah arose and went after

his wife, and came to the man and said to him, 'Are you the man who spoke to this woman?' And he said, 'I am.' And Manoah said, 'Now when your words come true, what is to be the boy's manner of life, and what is he to do?' And the angel of the Lord said to Manoah, 'Of all that I said to the woman let her beware. She may not eat of anything that comes from the vine, neither let her drink wine or strong drink, or eat any unclean thing; all that I commanded her let her observe.'

Manoah said to the angel of the Lord, 'Pray, let us detain you, and prepare a kid for you.' And the angel of the Lord said to Manoah, 'If you detain me, I will not eat of your food; but if you make ready a burnt offering, then offer it to the Lord.' (For Manoah did not know that he was the angel of the Lord.) And Manoah said to the angel of the Lord, 'What is your name, so that, when your words come true, we may honour you?' And the angel of the Lord said to him, 'Why do you ask my name, seeing it is wonderful?' So Manoah took the kid with the cereal offering, and offered it upon the rock to the Lord, to him who works wonders. And when the flame went up toward heaven from the altar, the angel of the Lord ascended in the flame of the altar while Manoah and his wife looked on; and they fell on their faces to the ground.

The angel of the Lord appeared no more to Manoah and to his wife. Then Manoah knew that he was the angel of the Lord. And Manoah said to his wife, 'We shall surely die, for we have seen God.'

The man who is open to the promptings of the Spirit within may experience God in nature, in another person, in a dream or a vision, in an encounter, in military defeat, or a bargain in the marketplace. Life is one, and indivisible, and the God of Israel presides over it all.

The second marker is one which was originally laid down by the great Marburg theologian Friedrich Heiler. The Book is called *Prayer* (OUP, 1932) and it makes the now familiar distinction between what he calls 'mystical' and 'prophetic' prayer. It is a crude distinction, which has to be qualified at many points, but a useful one for the beginner. Mystical religion, if I may be forgiven a gross abbreviation, is concerned with progress towards the ultimate vision of God, a process indeed initiated by God but depending for its fulfilment upon the steady and persistent withdrawal of the senses from the world, the practice of such asceticism as may be necessary, and a hunger and thirst for what always in this life lies ahead. For the prophet, on the other hand, the vision of God does not lie at the end of a long process, it is at the beginning of a long process, a process as the prophet sees it which is the ultimate practical sovereignty of God over all creation and over all human affairs. Our Lord Himself speaks of this ultimate as the Kingdom rather than the vision. This is an important distinction, however crude and unsatisfactory in the end, because it locates the essential religious activity not in what we do in pursuit of the vision, but what God has done already in His pursuit of us. 'Waiting, not seeking,' as Martin Buber puts it, 'we go our way.'

The third marker relates to feelings to which we are apt to pay undue attention. I rejoice as much as anyone else with those intimations of God's presence which very often are particularly prominent at the beginning of a man's Christian life, but when those feelings cease to charm, the unhappy pilgrim seems to be consumed with a fear that God has forsaken him, or that he has forsaken God, or that he has fallen off the spiritual ladder, or that he was perhaps mistaken in the first place anyway. Such cogitations are vain. The three apostles who accompanied our Lord to the Mount of Transfiguration were eager to preserve their feelings of awe and devotion and to set up three tabernacles as a memorial to the occasion. Instead, they found themselves, as they went down the mountain, listening to our Lord's warnings that this visionary experience on the mountain would be fulfilled through many years of toil and suffering and for some of them, martyrdom and death. 'Hitherto,' He said to Peter, 'You have girded yourself and gone wherever you have wanted to go, but the time is coming when another will gird you and take you where you have no desire to go' (John 21:18). It is a fearful thing to fall into the hands of the living God, by no means to be relished or sought for its own sake. Prayer is not always consolation or sweetness or light. There are times now when I would if I could evade the challenge of prayer altogether, live at the familiar levels, paddle in the shallows without ever going out into the deep. Prayer can be a very painful experience in which we become aware of our own emptiness and fragility and moral obloquy. As Henri Nouwen puts it in his book *Reaching Out* (Collins, 1976) – 'being useless and silent in the presence of our God belongs to the core of all prayer'. Or as Von Hügel puts it:

> In sufferings and dryness a more experienced soul can sustain the less. All deepened life is deepened to suffering, deepened to dreariness, deepened to joy. Dryness, dreariness and loneliness, east winds always blowing, desolation with certain lucid intervals and dim assurances.

When I first read those words as a very young Christian I thought them over-strained, exaggerated, the produce perhaps of too much spiritual refinement. But Von Hügel was right. The life of prayer does not offer easy solutions, it is not a comfortable cushion on which to settle down when life gets too difficult. The life of prayer, when it is real, exposes the pilgrim, as it did ancient Israel, to all the perils of the wilderness – that 'still wilderness' as Eckhart says 'where no man is at home'.

The preceding pages of this chapter have been concerned with the first question I was asked on Yorkshire Television – how do I know that God exists and is present? You have been reading one man's testimony to the existence and the presence of God. I am one amongst millions down the centuries, in every religious tradition, who can testify to the truth of it. But the prime witness is our Lord Himself. His life is not capable of interpretation, except against the background of a loving and well-tried faith in the existence and the presence of God. 'You hear me always,' He said.

The second question I was asked in the television studio was – 'Does prayer work?' It was a brash, but nevertheless important question and I now address myself to it at rather greater length than was possible within the course of a five-minute interview. In the first instance, I rely upon my own testimony, which is the only testimony I have. Yes, for me prayer does work – in terms of my own psychological needs. Looking back over my life I doubt whether I could have survived at all without those morning and evening spaces in which I slowly learnt to be quiet before God, in which I exposed my own angers and anxieties in His presence, when I listened to His word in the Bible and moved back into the mainstream of life refreshed, sometimes mortified, always grateful, for the gift of prayer.

But then we must not regard the life of prayer as an answer to our own psychological needs, real though they are. Does prayer 'work' in practical everyday matters? Does it procure peace out of war, health out of sickness, bread in the wilderness, water out of the hard rock, light in a dark place? I offer one simple illustration which must stand for a whole series of occasions on which, to my own mind, prayer did work. A fellow member of the RAF unit to which I belonged was told one evening that he was to be posted on the following day to a different unit. Both he and I, for perhaps different reasons, were both troubled at the decision, but there is no way in Service life of challenging that decision or even of deferring it. So with all the naivety of a young believer I prayed long and earnestly that evening that the decision should be changed – without in the least prescribing to the Good Lord how it should be done. The following morning the Commanding Officer called for us both and said, without any expression of surprise in his voice, 'Your posting has been cancelled, you are to stay here.' Is there a connection between those two events, divided only by a night's sleep? It has happened often enough in my own life, to be capable of no other explanation than that, to put it crudely, 'prayer does work'. But observe that one of the elements in prayer, often stressed in the Old Testament, and present in the New, is the element of waiting. Paul Tillich puts it like this in his book *The Shaking of the Foundations* (Penguin, 1949):

> We always have to wait for a human being. Even in the most intimate communion among human beings, there is an element of not having and not knowing, and of waiting. Therefore, since God is infinitely hidden, free, and incalculable, we must wait for Him in the most absolute and radical way. He is God for us just in so far as we do not possess Him.

Whether it be just for a night, or a week, or a year, or a lifetime, the echo in the voice of the psalmist:

> I wait for the Lord, my soul waits,
>   and in his word I hope;

my soul waits for the Lord
>more than watchmen for the morning,
>more than watchmen for the morning.

O Israel, hope in the Lord!
>For with the Lord there is steadfast love,
>and with him is plenteous redemption.

(Psalm 130:5–7)

But prayer is not to be valued simply in terms of what we receive, the victories we win, the gifts we acquire. In our Lord's view, and in the lives of the saints, prayer is a mighty weapon 'for the casting down of strongholds'. Those early saints who took themselves off to the desert did not do so primarily to escape the temptations or delusions of the civilized world to which they belonged. They did not believe that they were escaping from life, but rather engaging more fiercely in life at the very front line of the Christian mission – in the desert, where in contemporary opinion, the hosts of Satan ruled supreme. They were there to do battle, to cast down Satan's strongholds. When our Lord welcomed the disciples back after a successful mission of teaching and healing and casting out demons, He responded with one of the few notes of exultation which we are permitted to hear:

And he said to them, 'I saw Satan fall like lightning from heaven. Behold, I have given you authority to tread upon serpents and scorpions, and over all the power of the enemy; and nothing shall hurt you. Nevertheless do not rejoice in this, that the spirits are subject to you; but rejoice that your names are written in heaven.' (Luke 10:18–20)

The implication is that while they were busy in the streets and market places of Galilee, our Lord was far off, winning the battle in prayer. It will be obvious to the reader now, I trust, why we cannot regard prayer as a soft option, a way of escape, a way of getting money in the bank. He who comes to the Lord in this sense must prepare his soul for temptation. The man who thus engages with the powers of darkness is as sure of trouble as the sparks fly upwards.

But we need not depend on human testimony alone, fallible as it must often be. The life of prayer, when it is real, springs out of a theological conviction about, and a personal experience of, the goodness of God. I was asked to comment on a book, since published, under the title of *Good News of God* by E. M. Sidebottom (Darton, Longman and Todd, 1982). It is a book about the goodness of God; it abounds with felicitous illustrations from the Bible, showing how ingrained this conviction is in the hearts and minds of those who were the authors of the Bible. But the book springs out of personal experience as well – and not the kind of personal experience, you might imagine, which would lead a man to write about the goodness of God. The author, an experienced parish priest and a mature theologian, was himself in the grip of a serious illness. Yet the book glows with a sense of the goodness of God, with 'an ecstatic sense of the goodness of the universe':

> We are concerned with what the New Testament teaches, and the fact that there, and particularly in the Gospels, God's character is of paramount importance. We learn about reality in all sorts of ways, existential, political, scientific, but it is not really in doubt that the gospel is the touchstone. Christ is the incarnation of God. And the essence of the gospel is that God is goodness itself.

The author is not offering just a personal testimony to the experience of the goodness of God in his own life, he sees it as of the essence of the Scriptures, the 'characteristic feature of the gospel', the standard by which we judge all theology, the great spiritual fact of the universe which makes everything, be it disease, natural disaster, war, insanity, look different. The life of prayer is born of faith in the goodness of God, witnessed by the saints, testified to in Holy Scripture, and inseparable from the teaching of our Lord Himself. 'If you, being evil, know how to give good gifts to your children, how much more shall your Heavenly Father give good things to those who ask him' (Matthew 7:11).

I end with this striking quotation from chapter 5 of Mother Julian's *Revelations of Divine Love*, translated by Clifton Wolters (Penguin, 1973):

> It was at this time that our Lord showed me spiritually how intimately he loves us. I saw that he is everything that we know to be good and helpful. In his love he clothes

us, enfolds and embraces us; that tender love completely surrounds us, never to leave us. As I saw it he is everything that is good.

And he showed me more, a little thing, the size of a hazelnut, on the palm of my hand, round like a ball. I looked at it thoughtfully and wondered, 'What is this?' And the answer came, 'It is all that is made.' I marvelled that it continued to exist and did not suddenly disintegrate; it was so small. And again my mind supplied the answer, 'It exists, both now and for ever, because God loves it.' In short, everything owes its existence to the love of God.

In this 'little thing' I saw three truths. The first is that God made it; the second is that God loves it; and the third is that God sustains it. But what he is who is in truth Maker, Keeper, and Lover I cannot tell, for until I am essentially united with him I can never have full rest or real happiness; in other words, until I am so joined to him that there is absolutely nothing between my God and me. We have got to realize the littleness of creation and to see it for the nothing that it is before we can love and possess God who is uncreated. This is the reason why we have no ease of heart or soul, for we are seeking our rest in trivial things which cannot satisfy, and not seeking to know God, almighty, all-wise, all-good. He is true rest. It is his will that we should know him. Nothing less will satisfy us. No soul can rest until it is detached from all creation. When it is deliberately so detached for love of him who is all, then only can it experience spiritual rest.

God showed me too the pleasure it gives him when a simple soul comes to him, openly, sincerely and genuinely. It seems to me as I ponder this revelation that when the Holy Spirit touches the soul it longs for God rather like this; 'God, of your goodness give me yourself, for you are sufficient for me. I cannot properly ask anything less, to be worthy of you. If I were to ask less, I should always be in want. In you alone do I have all.'

Such words are dear indeed to the soul, and very close to the will and goodness of God. For his goodness enfolds every one of his creatures and all his blessed works, eternally and surpassingly. For he himself is eternity, and has made us for himself alone, has restored us by his blessed passion, and keeps us in his blessed love. And all because he is goodness.

ST MARK'S GOSPEL

Something absolutely marvellous happened in
Galilee 2000 years ago.

Alec McCowen (commenting on
his dramatized presentation
of St Mark's Gospel)

11 FAITH AND THE BIBLE

To read the Gospels, in a state of heightened consciousness and under unusual conditions, as I did in Heaton Park that Christmas-tide, is one thing; to attempt to read the whole Bible as I did in the wake of that experience is quite another thing. Enormous difficulties arise in the mind of the untutored. The obvious way to read the Bible seemed to me to follow from the obvious way in which we read any book – to start at the beginning and go through to the end. I am not the first, and indeed shall not be the last, to have made that attempt. I speak for myself alone when I say that this honest and arduous attempt began to flag half way through the book of Leviticus and expired altogether in the book of Numbers. Thereafter, by a merciful Providence, I was put in touch with the Bible Reading Fellowship and was enabled to find some sort of route through this labyrinthine literature. It never ceased to grip me, but it left me with many unanswered and indeed unanswerable questions which I was later to address as a student of theology, and subsequently as a teacher of theology.

The problems for the modern reader arise from the very nature of the literature itself. Some of the material can be traced back to a date round about the year 1500 B.C. And its very antiquity makes it obscure. Some of the words have no parallel either in other parts of the Bible or in contemporary literature; their meaning, therefore, can only be deduced from the context. Some of the allusions are to historical events of which we have no record; some of the metaphors arise out of a culture which we now only dimly apprehend. But to say, as I have done, that some of the material goes back as far as 1500 B.C. suggests another problem – we cannot be certain of the originating date of any book of the Bible, in the Old Testament or the New. We do not know, for the most part, who wrote the books of the Bible. Until comparatively recently the form in which the Bible was translated into English concealed the fact that we are here dealing with many different varieties of literature – prose and verse, for example; history and theology; court records and hymns; personal reflections and public exhortations; propaganda and philosophy. I ask you to imagine what a reader would feel like 2000 years hence who was presented with a composite volume which included *Pilgrim's Progress*, Rochester Cathedral Statutes, a selection of T. S. Eliot's poems, a few chapters from Gibbon's *Decline and Fall of the Roman Empire*, Bishop Robinson's *Honest to God*, *The Canterbury Tales*, Dag Hammarskjöld's diaries and Bede's ecclesiastical history. And imagine, more, that there are no chapter headings, no description of the conditions under which they were written, no mention of the authors, and no indication of how all these varied writings had come together in a single volume. This last question is the most perplexing of all when applied to the Bible – how did all these varied writings come together in a single volume, bound in black and entitled 'The Bible'.

So much for the problems of origination. Now (to use another technical term) what about transmission. I must explain what I am sure will be obvious to most readers, that we do not possess the original manuscripts of any single book of the Bible. They have long ago been lost, and it seems unlikely that any of them will ever be recovered. What we have instead are copies of the original manuscripts or tablets, which have been transmitted down the ages by a series of scholars and scribes whose names are wholly unknown. May I therefore attempt a thumbnail sketch of the process, which is of course capable of being challenged at any particular point. Let me take, for clarity's sake, the Torah, the five books of Moses, which we call the Pentateuch. The earliest productions, which now find their place within the totality of that book, were songs, transmitted orally from generation to generation, until at some unknown point they were incorporated in a longer text. Such would be the so-called Blessing of Jacob in Genesis 49, the songs of Moses and of Miriam in Exodus 15. It could be that the genealogies recorded here also go back to a long antiquity, because they were of great importance in establishing the later tribal organization of Israel. The narratives relating to the patriarchs, Moses and the exodus, and the wanderings in the wilderness, and the entry into the Promised Land, would have been conveyed in the first instance by word of mouth. Here is an example of this verbal transmission from Deuteronomy:

> When you come into the land which the Lord your God gives you for an inheritance, and have taken possession of it, and live in it, you shall take some of the first of all the fruit of the ground, which you harvest from your land that the Lord your God gives you, and you shall put it in a basket, and you shall go to the place which the Lord your God will choose, to make his name to dwell there. And you shall go the the priest who is in office at that time, and say to him, 'I declare this day to the Lord your God that I have come into the land which the Lord swore to our fathers to give us.' Then the priest shall take the basket from your hand, and set it down before the altar of the Lord your God.
>
> And you shall make response before the Lord your God, 'A wandering Aramean was my father; and he went down into Egypt and sojourned there, few in number; and there he became a nation, great, mighty, and populous. And the Egyptians treated us harshly, and afflicted us, and laid upon us hard bondage. Then we cried to the Lord the God of our fathers, and the Lord heard our voice, and saw our affliction, our toil, and our oppression; and the Lord brought us out of Egypt with a mighty hand and an outstretched arm, with great terror, with signs and wonders; and he brought us into this place and gave us this land, a land flowing with milk and honey. (26:1–9)

This is almost a perfect example of one way at least in which the history of the race was committed orally from generation to generation, from father to son. By the time the book of Deuteronomy was written the early history of the race had become part of the folklore of a nation.

If we ask the further question – at what point did all these separated materials come together in one narrative? – I can offer only the most tentative of suggestions. The art of writing was not widely disseminated and was confined, on the whole, to priests or, in later years, to scribes associated with some religious establishment or to the annalists at the royal court.

So certain records of the nation's history might have been preserved in Shiloh, in Dan or Samaria, or subsequently in Jerusalem. At this point in time, all that we have are traditions or writings associated with competing tribal or religious establishments. This is particularly obvious in the case of the Psalms where the use of particular phrases, and even the name for God, reflect varying practices at the different shrines of Israel. We can, I think, presume, although there is remarkably little evidence for it, that the process of the centralization of the literature of Israel, as it had gradually become, took a major step forward when in the reign of Josiah many of the country shrines were closed down and the worship of Israel became particularly associated with the Temple in Jerusalem. If there is a point at which the traditions of Israel begin to amalgamate, this is the most likely one. It was carried a stage further when Jerusalem was destroyed and a large part of the population was transported to Babylon. It was in Babylon where, with the Temple in ruins and the Davidic monarchy at an end, the people of Israel began to reconstitute their national life on the basis of a shared tradition and a common literature. There is little doubt that the Torah, or Pentateuch as we know it, took its final form during the exile in Babylon, and in some form became the basis of a new life in Jerusalem when some of the exiles returned there under Ezra the scribe. It was this book, the Pentateuch, now in a composite form, which became the basis of all subsequent Jewish life and remains so to this day. The second great section of the Old Testament as we know it – namely, the Prophets (which include 1 and 2 Samuel and 1 and 2 Kings) – came to be associated with the Torah and was regarded as an authoritative commentary on it. The rest of the Old Testament, as we have it – namely, the writings (which include Psalms, Proverbs, Chronicles, the wisdom writings) – came to share in the authority of the Torah as that was understood and interpreted in the 300 years or so before the birth of Christ.

I make no apology for this long excursus on the formation of the Old Testament, because it is often grossly misunderstood by Christian readers who are apt to put upon it interpretations which cannot on any grounds be sustained. The same process, although of course over a very much more limited period, has to be educed for the New Testament. The earliest documents of the New Testament are the Epistles of St Paul, which were preserved initially by the churches to which they were addressed, and subsequently acquired general authority in the Church as being the utterances of the great missionary apostle. The Gospels were a later development, taken in hand by several different authors when the apostolic era was coming to an end and few of the disciples of Christ on earth were still alive. St Mark is commonly regarded as the first of the Gospels and the reasons for its writing are indicated in this quotation from Eusebius, (previously cited) who is himself quoting Papias, a second century bishop of the Church:

> This also the presbyter used to say: Mark indeed, who became the interpreter of Peter, wrote accurately, as far as he remembered them, the things said or done by the Lord, but not however in order. For he had neither heard the Lord nor been His personal follower, but at a later stage, as I said, he had followed Peter, who used to adapt the teachings to the needs (of the moment), but not as though he were drawing up a connected account of the oracles of the Lord: so that Mark committed no error in writing certain matters just as he remembered them. For he had one object only in view, viz. to leave out nothing of the things which he had heard, and to include no false statement among them.*

The other Gospels arose either out of varying traditions in other centres of Christian life or in order to supplement what was regarded as the rather bare and fragmentary nature of the first Gospel. The public authority of these writings, Epistles and Gospels, arose from their association with the liturgy of the early Church and from their use by the early fathers of the Church in their conflict with heresy. The bulk of the New Testament was, so we believe, in general use and widely accepted by the year 130, and was later linked with the Old Testament in the way in which we are now familiar some time near the beginning of the third century. There were considerable doubts about some of the books of the New Testament, e.g. the book of the Hebrews, the Epistle of Jude, 2 Peter, 2 and 3 John and the Book of Revelation. By the end

*Quoted in A. E. J. Rawlinson, *The Gospel According to St Mark* (op. cit.).

of the fourth century, what we call the 'New Testament Canon' achieved its present form.

I have to say that all this was far from my mind (and perhaps fortunately so) when I struggled with the Bible in my latter years in the RAF, but then how could it be otherwise. St Augustine of Hippo was converted to the Christian faith by reading a verse from the Epistle to the Romans, but his subsequent writings over many years must bear witness to the continuing struggle as a preacher to comprehend and interpret the Sacred Scriptures as a whole and as a theologian to engage in the controversies which were so much part of his later life.

The Bible does not have to be understood in its totality before parts of it can speak powerfully to the individual seeker. As one wise man, Mark Twain I think, has said – 'It is not the parts of the Scripture that I don't understand that worry me, it is the parts that I do understand.'! The Bible has proved over the centuries its extraordinary power to awaken the mind, to challenge the spirit and to impose a new way of life upon the reader. But just to say that is to leave the reader dependent on his own experience, unarmed against the serious criticisms which can be urged against the Bible by those both within and outside the Church of God. If he is to remain a faithful servant, and indeed to become a faithful witness, he must come to grips with the problems and find a satisfying answer to them, which will transcend his own predilections and experiences. Even allowing for the fact that individual believers have found, as I have found, light and truth and new life in the pages of Scripture, how can we claim for the Scriptures any authority over and above the kind of authority which any great work of literature acquires in the course of history over the minds of its readers – the works of Shakespeare, for example, or of Dante, or of Aquinas, or of Karl Barth. It is to this question that I now address myself, and I can only proceed by way of illustration.

Carl Jung, in his *Memories, Dreams and Reflections* (Collins Fontana, 1967) tells the story of how he acquired some land at Bollingen in the Swiss Alps and there proceeded, in 1922, to build himself a house which he called 'The Tower'. In subsequent years he added to, and reconstructed the house in a variety of ways, more particularly after his wife died in 1955. He offers in his book good psychological reasons why he built in the way he did. For him it was a unity arising out of and expressing his deepest innermost needs. But to the outsider it must have seemed a strangely ramshackle construction, built haphazardly over the years, entirely lacking the kind of facilities which any modern house might be expected to have. Carl Jung was neither an architect nor a builder by profession, and the construction left a lot to be desired. If any of his visitors had been rude enough thus to comment on his house I suppose he would have said that such details meant nothing to him. He was not concerned that the windows might not be straight, or were ill-proportioned. What mattered to him was the view over the lake, which brought solace to a sorely troubled mind and (this is important) was unique. No other house could ever again command such a view. It was his alone.

Some such analogy might be applied, with profit, to the Bible. It is, so the critics would urge, a ramshackle construction, without seemingly any central purpose; it has within it many obvious, many more less obvious, contradictions which arise from the nature of its growth; its acceptance in the Church was partial, and as a base for the great doctrinal edifices of the Christian faith, wholly unconvincing; it purveys moral attitudes which are wholly alien to a cultivated moral sense; it records savageries which we would be better to forget; by its very diversity it has created divisions not only in the Christian Church but in Judaism. It is, in short, but a thing of shreds and patches, with no authoritative message for the contemporary world. Yes, we would have to agree to that. Like every other clergyman, I was subjected to such considerations at theological college and university, and subsequently as a teacher of theology myself, subjected my own students to such considerations. But my reply to them would be the kind of reply I put on the lips of Carl Jung when his own ramshackle house was criticized – it is the view that matters.

The remarkable thing about the Bible is that for all the varieties of literature within it, the range of time which it covers and the number of authors who have contributed to it, it still offers what seems to me a convincing and certainly unique view of human existence. This is all the more remarkable when you consider that the authors were sometimes divided by centuries, had never met, and were by and large wholly unaware of the other writings which were ultimately to constitute the canon of Holy Scripture. No serious attempt was made to iron out the differences, remove the contradictions or to establish a notional unity. The view of human existence which it offers can be represented in two theological statements. The first is the uncompromising goodness of God. And the second is the painful destiny of man.

At first sight it is difficult to see how that first statement can possibly be substantiated. All the evidence of the Old Testament at least seems to run the other way – the story of the flood and the destruction of the human race; the bizarre, devastating punishment inflicted on the Egyptians by the plagues; the bloody battles and the blatant deceptions of the wilderness period; the destruction of the cities of Canaan, and the genocide which accompanied it; the ridiculous aspirations and the painful disappointments of the Chosen People; the repeated subjugations at the hands of foreign powers, and the ultimate disappearance of all but one of the tribes of Israel. Can all this be compatible, we may well ask, with 'the goodness of God'. And what about our own experience? Not just the great national and personal disasters, or the ravages of age and disease, or even man's inhumanity to man expressed in a thousand different ways, but the painful, tiresome accidents of everyday existence which diminish us and destroy our confidence in life.

In a previous chapter I have shown how important a belief in the goodness of God is to the whole inner life of the Christian. But observe that I have added the word 'uncompromising', and this is perhaps a clue to our better understanding of the Old Testament. The prophet Hosea, one of the most sensitive and perceptive of the Hebrew prophets, himself greatly sinned against in his own domestic life, is one of the most impressive exponents of 'the goodness of God'. Nevertheless, in that same book the yearning love of God for His people is matched by an equally fierce denunciation of their sins. The goodness of God is 'uncompromising', demanding justice, fair dealing, honest worship, loving concern for others, and therefore seemingly harsh in His pursuit of this ideal for the human race. The figure of God as Father, so often delineated both in the Old Testament and in the New, is not intended to suggest the kind of easy-going father who simply provides security for his children or indulges their whims. The Jewish father was never like this; he was concerned more than anything else with ensuring that his son embraced the faith of his ancestors and walked in the way of the law. He was prepared to exercise a fierce discipline in the procuring of those ends. The 'father-figure' of the contemporary world bears little relationship to the father-figure of the ancient world or the father-figure of our Lord's teaching. So we have to measure God's dealings with us as with others, by the standard of His uncompromising concern to establish goodness in the world and to abolish evil. Therefore 'Let him who comes to the Lord prepare his soul for trials'.

Associated with the uncompromising goodness of God is the 'painful destiny of man'. This is perhaps as surprising as the assertion of the uncompromising goodness of God. For, so the casual reader is led to believe, the Bible has a poor view of mankind, fallen from grace and destined, unless he is very fortunate, for eternal punishment. The story of the Fall in Genesis 3 seems to convey the same message. But the drift of the story is in fact quite the other way. Man is destined for natural easy intercourse with his creator, who 'walks in the garden in the cool of the evening'. He is destined to live, as the author of Job puts it, 'in league with the stones of the field and to be at peace with the beasts of the field' (Job 5:23). The picture of the Garden of Eden is not of some prehistoric paradise, but of some future state either within or beyond history to which mankind painfully aspires. It would be easier for him if he were a cow or a dog, without these uncomfortable aspirations, content to live for the day, satisfied with food and shelter. But the inner history of mankind reveals that this is not so. His secret pain, seldom diagnosed, arises from his desire for eternal life with God in the garden. I know of no better expression of this 'painful destiny' outside of Holy Scripture than in Edwin Muir's poem 'Outside Eden'*:

A few lead in their harvest still
By the ruined wall and broken gate.
Far inland shines the radiant hill.
Inviolable the empty gate,
Impassable the gaping wall;
And the mountain over all.

*From Edwin Muir, *Collected Poems*, Faber, 1964.

Such is the country of this clan,
Haunted by guilt and innocence.

These two poles of biblical theology are never very far apart,
reference to one or the other would be found in every book
and in every documentary tradition of the Bible. It would be
an interesting exercise for a Bible-study group to look for this
view of life in any book to which it may turn. They are never
very far apart; when they approximate to each other in the
human mind, then faith becomes a possibility.

But as I have said, these considerations were far from me
when I first began my studies in the Bible. I can only testify,
as a student and as an expositor of the Bible, to its remarkable
power still to evoke the presence of God. Sir Edwin Hoskins
once said of his own studies that 'he began with his head in
a lexicon and ended at the throne of God'. In a modest way
that has been my continuing experience as each day I try to
bend my mind to the sacred text. P. T. Forsyth,* the famous
theologian of the earlier part of this century, put it this way:

> There is an autonomy and finality in the Bible for faith.
> Experience in this region does not mean a prior standard
> in us by which we accept or reject the Gospel's claims. It
> does not mean that the Gospel submits to be tried by the
> code we have put together from our previous experience of
> natural things, even in the religious sphere. The Gospel is
> not something which is there for our assent in the degree
> in which we can verify it by our previous experience either
> in the way of need or of rationality. Our very response to
> it is created in us before it is confessed by us. It creates
> assent rather than accepts it. The experience in which our
> final authority emerges and is recognised, as the servants
> know their true lord, is the soul's leap to its touch. It is
> not a conclusion but a venture of faith.

Yes, the authority of the Bible rests in the end in 'the soul's
leap to its touch'. It is put another way in a more recent book
by Prebendary Cleverley Ford, entitled *The Ministry of the
Word* (Hodder and Stoughton, 1978):

*In *The Principle of Authority*, London Independent Press, 1913.

I. T. Ramsey asserted that the Bible presents a distinctly 'odd' or 'improper' kind of language because it handles those peculiar kinds of situations in which 'the penny drops' and which 'come alive' offering both discernment and commitment. They are disclosure situations. The significance of the language of the Bible therefore which handles them is not the facts underlying the narrative, nor even the event plus interpretation, but the events as disclosure points of what, in the last resort, we can only call God. Language then discloses, it even brings into being ultimate meaning or ultimate reality. So the 'odd' language of the Bible is able to be a means of making possible the real presence of God.

The academic arguments I have been propounding in this chapter will not make the reader believe in the Bible nor make him a successful apologist for it, unless and until he finds himself in what Ian Ramsey called the 'disclosure situation', in which mind and heart long for the living water and meet One who is able to draw that water from a deep well which we call, for want of a better term, 'the Bible'.

AGNOSTICISM

. . . you will ask me, 'How am I to think of God himself, and what is he?' and I cannot answer you except to say 'I do not know!' For with this question you have brought me into the same darkness, the same cloud of unknowing where I want you to be! For though we through the grace of God can know fully about all other matters, and think about them – yes, even the very works of God himself – yet of God himself can no man think. Therefore I will leave on one side everything I can think and choose for my love that thing which I cannot think! Why? Because he may well be loved, but not thought. By love he can be caught and held, but by thinking never.

Anonymous – 14th century
(*The Cloud of Unknowing*, tr. C. Wolters, Penguin, 1961)

The most satisfying and ecstatic faith is almost purely agnostic. It trusts absolutely without professing to know at all.

(H. L. Mencken)

12   FAITH AND MYSTERY

I have written a book about 'living by faith', a book with the same title could have been written by a Muslim, a Jew or a Hindu. You will have presumed that a priest in the Church of England who writes a book about living by faith is living by faith in Christ. That is the assumption I have made all the way through, but the time has come to justify it.

I began living by faith under the impact of an experience which I have already described, which is by its very nature, incommunicable. What happened to me happened below the level of intellectual awareness, although inevitably it issued in the end in certain intellectual convictions. The Gospels which I read were simply at hand; they had a certain aura imparted by long association with worship and culture; I believed in them because I had no reason not to believe in them; I alighted upon a treasure in an unexpected place where I had never thought of looking for it before. Forty years later, with a good deal of study and teaching now behind me, I have come to the conclusion that my faith in the Gospels was justified. The Christ I encountered in them was, so I believe, a real person, living in a real world which can be described and analysed. The easy scepticism with which New Testament scholarship in the early part of this century treated the Gospel narratives, is no longer as prominent or as persuasive as it seemed. To take one example, alluded to by Anthony Harvey in his book *Jesus and the Constraints of History* (Duckworth, 1982). Some of my readers will not know that even the designation 'Jesus of Nazareth' has sometimes been in doubt. No such place name occurs in the Old Testament, no inscriptions are available bearing the name, and so it was possible to deduce that the place name was a theological construction by the author associated with the Old Testament office of 'Nazirite'. An interesting theory indeed, but then in archaeological excavations in 1955 it was discovered that there was indeed a town of that name well before the Christian era, and in 1961 an inscription was discovered in Caesarea bearing the name of Nazareth. I quote now from Anthony Harvey's book:

> This little episode by no means stands alone. It is symptomatic of the way in which archaeology has tended in recent years to enhance the credibility of the gospel narratives. A conspicuous instance of this, though it is still not widely known, is a discovery that was made some ten years ago by Israeli archaeologists in a burial ground just outside Jerusalem. It was the custom of the Jews, some years after the burial of a corpse in a tomb of rock, to gather the bones of the deceased and preserve them in small stone boxes called ossuaries. One of these ossuaries, dating from the first century A.D., was found in a cemetery on the Mount of Olives, and contained the bones of a man named Jehohanan who had died in his mid-twenties and who had apparently been crucified. The nail which had been driven through his anklebones to secure him to the cross had evidently proved impossible to remove and was still in place, with fragments of wood adhering to it. The bones of the lower part of the legs had been broken by a transverse blow.
>
> Here, then, is totally independent evidence for the crucifixion of a contemporary of Jesus. In a number of significant details – the nail, the breaking of the legs – it agrees precisely with the account given in the gospels. That is to say; it is no longer possible (if it ever was) to regard the gospel narratives as pious legend or irresponsible fabrication.

This is a telling comment because in fact Anthony Harvey is not primarily in business for sustaining the historicity of the Gospels; the book is concerned, as the title suggest, with the political, religious and social constraints to which Jesus was subject. So, apparently in the Gospels we do have a reliable, if far from complete, narrative concerning the life and death and resurrection of a young Jewish man who was brought up in Nazareth, who preached his first sermon in a synagogue in Nazareth, who gathered to Himself a group of disciples, some of whom had been followers of His cousin, John the Baptist, who attracted a good deal of attention in His native Galilee, was credited with some striking miracles of healing, who provoked opposition even there from the official leaders of Judaism, who went on pilgrimage to Jerusalem, was arrested, tried and condemned to death.

So far the story could be the story of many another social or religious pioneer who ran foul of the establishment and paid the price for his temerity. If that were all, we would look back on the life of Jesus with the kind of admiration we have for Socrates or Galileo or Dietrich Bonhoeffer. He might have earned a chapter in a book on liberation theology and that would be all. But there are, so we are told, some 1,500 million Christians in the world, some of whom in varying degrees of intensity, subscribe to the words of the Nicene Creed:

> We believe in one Lord Jesus Christ, the only begotten Son of God, begotten of his Father before all worlds, God of God, Light of Light, Very God of Very God, begotten not made, being of one substance with the Father, by whom all things were made.

With these words we pass beyond the bounds of sober historical enquiry and we proclaim a mystery.

The word 'mystery' needs some explanation. In current usage it can be applied to an unsolved murder, to a ride in the country without route or destination, to the appearance of a UFO in your neighbour's back garden, or in short, to any event which defies explanation in terms which are available to us. St Paul uses the word mystery in a rather different sense. He speaks of the 'mystery of the Gospel', 'the mystery of God', a divine purpose which has been kept hidden from former ages and has been made known in the fullness of times through Christ; the mystery of the inclusion of the Gentiles as well as of the Jews in the divine purpose. This is 'mystery' in the sense not that it eludes the intellect but that it overwhelms it; it is not capable of comprehension in more enlightened days, it is incapable of comprehension with the kind of mental apparatus available to us. So while there is a close connection between the Jesus of history and the Christ enthroned in heaven, the relationship between them is a mystery. And although it is indubitably true that Jesus was a man, born in a particular place at a particular time, brought up within a particular family and subject to the constraints of history, it is also regarded as indubitably true by the Church that He was more than a man. The Nicene Creed does not explain the mystery, it simply proclaims it, in language which wholly transcends the minds of the author of the Creed and of those who, Sunday after Sunday, recite it in the churches of Christendom.

A sense of mystery is inseparable from the Christian faith, and those who find the Creeds difficult or Christian dogmas incomprehensible are in exactly the same position as those who formed the Creeds or articulated the dogmas. The formularies of the Church do little more than illustrate the ways in which men of a previous generation, in their own bewilderment, expressed the mystery. This is an uncomfortable view for the Christian who looks for unchanging Christian doctrines, for intellectual security, for a comfortable mental environment. No such securities are available to mortal man – we walk by faith and not by sight. What I experienced when I first read the Gospels was not a happy resolution of all my intellectual problems, but a sense of the overwhelming power of God present in the life and death and resurrection of Jesus of Nazareth. It has ever been so – Abraham experienced God in a horror of darkness, Jacob experienced God in that mysterious struggle by the ford Jabbock where he was not vouchsafed even the name of God, and Job found God not in the animadversions of his so-called comforters, the conventional teachers of Israel, but in an ineffable awareness of his own finitude and insignificance before his Creator.

Then the Lord answered Job out of the whirlwind:
'Who is this that darkens counsel by words without
          knowledge?
Gird up your loins like a man,
    I will question you, and you shall declare to me.

'Where were you when I laid the foundation of the earth?
    Tell me, if you have understanding.
Who determined its measurements – surely you know!
    Or who stretched the line upon it?
On what were its bases sunk,
    or who laid its cornerstone,

when the morning stars sang together,
  and all the sons of God shouted for joy?

'Or who shut in the sea with doors,
  when it burst forth from the womb;
when I made clouds its garment,
  and thick darkness its swaddling band,
and prescribed bounds for it,
  and set bars and doors,
and said, 'Thus far shall you come, and no farther,
  and here shall your proud waves be stayed'?

'Have you commanded the morning since your days began,
  and caused the dawn to know its place,
that it might take hold of the skirts of the earth,
  and the wicked be shaken out of it?
It is changed like clay under the seal,
  and it is dyed like a garment.
From the wicked their light is withheld,
  and their uplifted arm is broken.

'Have you entered into the springs of the sea,
  or walked in the recesses of the deep?
Have the gates of death been revealed to you,
  or have you seen the gates of deep darkness?
Have you comprehended the expanse of the earth?
  Declare, if you know all this.'

                                                    (Job 38:1–18)

Living by faith is no easy option; it does not provide all
the answers, it does not solve all the problems. In fact, living
by faith is the harder option; it confronts us with a mystery
which will not yield to human intellect, however well tutored,
or to human imagination, however adventurous.

Perhaps I could be permitted a kind of diversion which yet
bears upon the subject of this chapter, and it arises out of my
own experience. The observer of a clergyman's life might be
forgiven for thinking that it consists of taking services,
preaching sermons, visiting homes, writing articles for the
parish magazine, talking to troubled people in his study,
preparing young men and women for marriage, consoling the
aged in their distress, then performing the last sad rites to
those whose journey in this world is over. That is demanding

enough, in all conscience, as anyone who undertakes it in
response to the call of God finds to his cost. But the real
burden of ministry is invisible, known only to the man himself.
He is one who lives by faith, but by faith in a mystery which
he can never articulate satisfactorily for himself, or explain
satisfactorily to his congregation. It is not simply that his
mental equipment is not adequate to the task, or that he
is not a good communicator, or that his congregation are
indifferent to truth. It is that both the minister and his congregation are at the mercy of an overwhelming truth which no
one has ever or will ever penetrate this side of the grave. The
story of the professor and his pupil is an instructive one –
'Do you understand it,' the professor said; 'then you've got
it wrong.' The comforters depicted in the story of Job had all
the answers, so they supposed; they were the official teachers
of Israel and had been well instructed in the faith. But it was
the heretic, Job himself, who was rewarded with the vision
of God and walked into the light.

All this seems far removed from the Gospels – but it is not
so. I draw your attention to an instructive passage in St
Matthew's Gospel:

> Now when Jesus came into the district of Caesarea Philippi,
> he asked his disciples, 'Who do men say that the Son of
> man is?' And they said, 'Some say John the Baptist, others
> say Elijah, and others Jeremiah or one of the prophets.' He
> said to them, 'But who do you say that I am?' Simon Peter
> replied, 'You are the Christ, the Son of the living God.'
> And Jesus answered him, 'Blessed are you, Simon Bar-
> Jona! For flesh and blood has not revealed this to you, but
> my Father who is in heaven.' (16:13–17)

This is sometimes regarded as a crucial passage for the notion
of Petrine supremacy but it is in fact far more than an ecclesiastical proof text. It is a demonstration of the sense of mystery
which pervaded our Lord's relationship even with His earliest
followers. The impact of our Lord upon His contemporary
society inevitably provoked the question, 'Who is He?' The
instinctive response of the Jew would be to associate Him
with the prophets, i.e. a man of God, operating by the distinct
authority of God and proclaiming His word. But some of
them were more specific. When they saw Jesus in action they

thought of Elijah, and some thought of Jeremiah. But observe the strange incompatibility of these two figures from the past. Elijah was a fervent nationalist, deeply involved in politics, who stood before kings unafraid, who took the battle to the prophets of Baal and won a mighty victory, who performed miracles and finally ascended into heaven. It was a dramatic life, violent, seemingly unpredictable, strange to the ordinary ways of men. Contrast Jeremiah, a timid shrinking man, who made no great impact on his contemporaries, who knew himself to be a feeble speaker, somewhat short (so the narrative suggests) on physical courage, and furthermore a dissident, a traitor, who went out to the armies of Babylon. Jesus, it seems, combined in His own life and ministry all these seemingly incompatible elements to such an extent that His hearers could associate Him with either one or the other without seeming contradiction. Peter himself, it is true, went one stage further and under pressure of questioning by our Lord enunciated his faith in Him as the Christ, or the Messiah.

And yet even this ascription was not without ambiguity, both in his own mind and in the minds of the other disciples. What sort of Messiah was He? Would He mobilize His followers in a fight to the death with the Roman authorities? Would He take His followers with Him to some remote Qumran, there to await the end of the world? Would He come with the clouds of heaven proclaiming the kingdom of God? Even to acknowledge Christ as the Messiah, without further qualification, was the result of an act of God, not a deliverance of human wisdom. Already those early followers were feeling the weight of the mystery with which the person of Christ was invested. Other writers of the New Testament when they approach the mystery, express their wondering bewilderment in a variety of titles, which only serve to describe the overwhelming impact of this little Jewish man from Nazareth – the second Adam, the alpha and the omega, the cornerstone, the day-star, the high priest, the image of God, the bread of life, the Lamb of God, the mediator, the Prince of Peace, the Redeemer, the Saviour, the servant, the Son of Man, the Truth, the vine, the Way, the Word. Like the credal affirmations of a later age, these titles proclaim, without ever explaining, the mystery.

You must not be surprised, dear reader, if you find the preaching in your local church unconvincing. The preacher is simply following in the steps of those before him, whose minds have collapsed before the Christ, the child of Nazareth who fills the universe. You would have a right to be surprised if the preacher were confident, assured of the truth, able to articulate it in plain matter-of-fact language, if he could capture the Christ in some category of his own, as a political figure or an appealing teacher, or a simple man of the people, or the object of a cult, or the charismatic leader. He understands it all? – he has got it wrong. He is no follower of the apostles.

One of the earliest sketches of Vincent Van Gogh is called 'En Route'. H. R. Graetz says, in his book, *The Symbolic Language of Vincent Van Gogh* (Thames and Hudson, 1963) that: 'This clumsy little drawing already portrays all the important elements of his life.' It is the picture of an unprepossessing figure, wearing the inevitable huge boots which we associate with Van Gogh's work, walking on a country road with a lamp in his hand. The only other features of the landscape are a tree, bare and spiky, and in the distance a house with the windows faintly illuminated. No language, of course, can do justice to the power of Van Gogh's visual imagery. It does tell the story of his life – the lonely man who has come a long way and has still a long way to go, with a lamp in his hand to light the next step, with only the faintly illuminated windows in the distance. It could have been, if Van Gogh's life had developed in a different way, the picture of a man 'living by faith'. He does not see very far, the road is very long and very hard. The environment is threatening, the shadows deep, the illumination slight. But he walks – in those big boots of his, not indeed an heroic figure, but a plodder doing the only thing he knows how to do. He has a painful history behind him, he has no exciting stories to tell, he walks alone – but ahead is the glory.

It is difficult not to end a book about 'living by faith' without quoting this magnificent passage from *Pilgrim's Progress*, which will have revived many a pilgrim as he labours towards the Celestial City, sustained in much weariness only by faith in the living God, who called him to the journey and will welcome His pilgrim home at the end of it:

After this it was noised abroad that Mr Valiant-for-Truth was sent for by summons by the same post as the other, and had this for a token that the summons was true, 'That his pitcher was broken at the fountain.' (Eccles. xii. 6.) When he understood it, he called for his friends, and told them of it. Then said he, I am going to my Father's; and though with great difficulty I have got hither, yet now I do not repent me of all the troubles I have been at to arrive where I am. My sword I give to him that shall succeed me in my pilgrimage, and my courage and skill to him that can get it. My marks and scars I carry with me, to be a witness for me that I have fought His battles who now will be my rewarder. When the day that he must go hence was come, many accompanied him to the river-side, into which as he went he said, 'Death, where is thy sting?' And as he went down deeper, he said, 'Grave, where is thy victory?' So he passed over, and all the trumpets sounded for him on the other side.

THE KEY

Faith changes the face of the earth; by it the heart is raised, entranced and becomes conversant with heavenly things. Faith is our light in this life. By it we possess the truth without seeing it; we touch what we cannot feel, and see what is not evident to the senses. By it we view the world as though it did not exist. It is the key of the treasure house, the key of the abyss of the science of God. It is faith that teaches us the hollowness of created things; by it God reveals and manifests Himself in all things. By faith the veil is torn aside to reveal the eternal truth.

> J.-P. de Caussade (*Self-Abandonment to Divine Providence*, 1750, Ramière, 1921)

CONCLUSION

It is time to complete the circle, and turn back to the question raised by the incident which I described in the introduction – what is the strange impulse by which the language of assent is replaced by the language of faith, by which adherence to a religious body is replaced by the power to move mountains, to heal the sick, to cause the lame to walk, stop the mouths of lions, to cast down strongholds? In the preceding chapters of this book I have walked round the question and have viewed it from many angles. The time has come to attempt the answer, and in so doing inevitably to expose the poverty of my understanding.

In most of the rich spiritual experience recorded in Holy Scripture there are two invariable factors compounded together in this transition from assent to faith. The experiences so described, alike in the Old Testament and the New, are all within the context of what we may call 'the Church'; Jacob, Moses, Samuel, Isaiah, Job, Nehemiah, the disciples of Christ, Paul, James, were all members of the Chosen People, already believers in the Living God, and in some cases holders of office within the Covenant People. They had, in varying degrees, assented to the faith of their fathers; all of them were called to make the transition from assent to faith, and in each case the transition was made on the basis of revelation and obedience. Moses was vouchsafed a vision of the Living God at the burning bush, which was followed by a positive and painful act of obedience – go back to Egypt. Isaiah, no stranger to the Temple, was caught up into a vision of the ineffable God in heaven and responded in tones of awed submission – 'Here am I, send me'. The three apostles on the Mount of Transfiguration were immediately warned of the cost of their obedience and followed Christ down into a world bent on His destruction and theirs. In St Paul's account of his own conversion he associates vision and obedience within a single sentence – 'Wherefore, O King Agrippa, I was not disobedient to the heavenly vision' (Acts 26:19). The point is nowhere better put than by George MacDonald in his *Unspoken Sermons* (2nd series, Longmans Green, 1886):

Do you ask, 'What is faith in him?' I answer, The leaving of your way, your objects, your self, and the taking of his and him; the leaving of your trust in men, in money, in opinion, in character, in atonement itself, and doing as he tells you. I can find no words strong enough to serve for the weight of this necessity – this obedience. It is the one terrible heresy of the church, that it has always been presenting something else than obedience as faith in Christ.

The story associated with Erasmus of a conversation with the Pope of his day lives on to haunt every great ecclesiastical structure. The Pope said, as he showed his visitor the glories of the Vatican – 'We can no longer say "silver and gold have I none".' 'No,' said his visitor, 'but then you cannot say either "in the name of Christ stand up and walk".' But there are those who can say 'stand up and walk', there are those who have yielded in themselves to the strange alchemy of revelation and obedience. It is they who in the secret places of the earth, often unseen by men, through faith conquer kingdoms, enforce justice, gain strength out of weakness, put armies to flight – of whom the world is not worthy. When I stood in the room of my crippled parishioner in my first country parish I was an official of the Church, ordained to the Sacred ministry, modestly equipped with a knowledge of theology, able to assent with enthusiasm to the Creed I had embraced. I was not entirely without the 'silver and gold' bequeathed to me by a long religious tradition – but I lacked the power to say 'stand up and walk'. At that moment I was not required to scale the heights of faith, essayed by Jacob and Moses, and Samuel and Paul. Perhaps I was being asked in that moment to submit to a vision and on the strength of it to obey. Not all visions are of an exciting or invigorating kind. They sometimes leave the heart cold and dull and chastened. I take such comfort as I can from the story of the agonized father suddenly confronted with the possibility of healing for his demented child, who cried to Christ out of his agony of love and longing – 'I believe, help my unbelief' (Mark 9:24).

I have not answered my question, nor indeed shall I ever do so. It is one of the mysteries of existence by which assent is turned into faith, by which adherence becomes power. Meanwhile, I can only testify to the joyful and (when not joyful) creative experience of 'living by faith'.

INDEX